$15.95

salary
Management
for the
Nonspecialist

Stanley B. Henrici

Salaried workers account for an increasing proportion of total compensation in the U.S.A. as our nation evolves into a service economy. Projections for 1985 indicate that white-collar employees will outnumber blue-collar workers by more than 60 percent. As supervisors, managers are constantly beset by questions about salary and why the compensation system works as it does. Recently passed EEO legislation has introduced another dimension—possible charges of salary discrimination.

Then there are the questions of employee morale and turnover. If the salary system is perceived as arbitrary or inequitable, desirable employees often vote with their feet, further adding to the organization's costs. This book is a primer on salary administration designed for managers in smaller organizations who often must set up and administer salary programs on their own. Managers in larger organizations with professional salary administrators will find it useful when answering those inevitable employee questions about salary, because it explains in everyday language the seemingly arbitrary rules and conventions of salary management.

Salary Management for the Nonspecialist

STANLEY B. HENRICI

amacom

A division of
AMERICAN MANAGEMENT ASSOCIATIONS

Library of Congress Cataloging in Publication Data

Henrici, Stanley B
  Salary management for the nonspecialist.

  Includes index.
  1. Compensation management. I. Title.
HF5549.5.C67H47   658.3'2   80-65877
ISBN 0-8144-5565-4

© 1980 AMACOM

A division of American Management Associations, New York.

FIRST PRINTING

CONTENTS

1	INTRODUCTION	1
2	SALARY POLICY	9
3	JOB EVALUATION	30
4	SALARY STRUCTURE	64
5	SALARY RANGE	84
6	SALARY SURVEYS	100
7	COMPARATIO	124
8	APPRAISALS	141
9	SALARY INCREASES	158
10	SALARY BUDGETING	186
11	SALARY CONTROL	206
12	THE SALARY ETHIC	224
Index		235

1: INTRODUCTION

As an executive you may have noticed that dealing with fixed expenses is like trying to thin out a school of minnows by hand. The things are there and visible, but when you try to get hold of them, they are surprisingly elusive. You may reach down and churn the water and pull out a few slow movers, but as soon as you have withdrawn your hand, there the school is, as large and active as ever.

Of all fixed expenses the salary account can be the most troublesome and difficult to get hold of. There is a looseness in it. It is not like the hourly payroll, which is clearly defined by the union contract, agreed to on a known date, and operative till another known date. For each hourly job the rates of pay are predictable, and the number of jobs is controllable through work-measured standards.

Not so the salary payroll. Except in a salary-union company, hiring rates are determined by the negotiations of the moment: people are recruited throughout the year in an individual bargaining process. As for salary increases, they never loom large when they occur. In many companies they lodge themselves in the payroll, not at one time when they can be seen en masse, but in any and every month. Presumably they are based on good judgment. But how can you be sure? Are they for merit or for cost of living? A nagging feeling that the whole salary area is mysterious and vague—more like a school of darting fish than like a single sailfin that can be gaffed at the end of a line—this feeling can bedevil the executive responsible for the cost of running an enterprise.

This vagueness is especially puzzling because the subject of salary administration seems to be straightforward. Pay people the proper rate for what they do. Give them increases as necessary. Be fair. But again, questions. How do you know what constitutes a "proper" salary for what someone is doing? Proper by what yardstick? As for increases, under what circumstances do they have to be given? And how do you decide on the amount? Much of this boils down to fairness. But again, fair to whom? The employee? The employer? Both? Fair in what sense?

Way back when, salaries were not considered to be much of a problem. It was in the hourly payroll, not the salary payroll, that the great drifts of employee expense piled up. Many techniques were worked out to control these expenses. Predetermined time standards, crew specifications, job evaluation, pay scales, seniority rules—a host of formalized procedures governed the management of hourly pay. That was where the money was. Salaries, on the other hand, went to relatively few people. They weren't a major cost element. And such attention as they did get was personalized and relatively informal. Today things are different.

Salary pay is now a major channel of employee expense outlays. By 1950, white-collar workers had pulled abreast of blue-collar workers in numbers. By 1976, they led the blue-collar corps by 50 percent. By 1985, the differential will have risen to 60 percent. Clearly, the management and control of white-collar salaries demands increasing care, both for the containment of the bulky costs involved and for equitable treatment of the large number of people affected.

Such consideration is by no means absent among employers, but it varies in degree. Thus, in ascending order of control, we may list various stages in the administration of salaries:

1. Salary actions handled on an ad hoc basis, with each individual treated according to circumstances.
2. Informal salary determination, but with rules and guidelines to govern the frequency and amount of increases.
3. Job ranking or classification systems and formalized job salary scales, implemented through rules and guidelines as in item 2.
4. Salary policies and salary surveys, together with the administrative elements of item 3.
5. Salary management, including attention to the purpose of, need for, and interrelationship among salaried positions in order to control salary costs, together with all the elements of item 4.

Items 2, 3, and 4 primarily address the procedures for dealing with salaries in the organization. They constitute what is commonly called *salary administration.* Item 5 goes further: it concerns itself with the number of salaries in the organization. In this way, it looks at total salary expense and supplies methods for governing it. When control has reached this stage, it is termed *salary management.*

This classification is by no means perfect, for certainly there are overlaps. Most large employers have reached stage 4 and many are experiencing success in stage 5. Some small establishments are at stage 5 in the control of the number of salaried jobs but are not yet out of stage 1 in the control of individual salaries.

Small employers—those having, say, from 10 to 500 salaried employees—must especially emphasize clarity on salary thinking. If the national trend is reflected in your firm, salaries are a growing proportion of total expense. Worse, unlike direct labor, they do not fluctuate with the ups and downs of business. They are fixed, and if they become too heavy they will sink your ship below an invisible Plimsoll line called "breakeven." At the same time, in the small firm the difficulties of keeping track of salary actions cannot, as in a large company, be entrusted to a specialized department. There are not enough bodies to justify the expense.

Often, then, it is the top executive of the small establishment who handles salary matters as a part-time job. Or perhaps, going a step further, the top executive leaves such matters to supervisors, subject to review and approval. Or, a little further still, the executive relies on the budget, simple guidelines, or delegation to a personnel manager for control.

For establishments that are large enough to have salaried employees reporting to supervisors under a president or general manager, diffusion of salary control, even under central guidance, does not erase problems from the slate. Rather, it chalks up new ones.

For example, supervisors have diverse and often conflicting objectives. Some of them are stingy and would, if they had their way, hold all their employees to rock-bottom wages in the face of the largesse offered by company policy. Others feel that the best way to keep costs down is to pay people well, especially the most deserving. At lunch, when they have cornered their boss, they explain that if they were freed from the shackles of salary control, they could hire expert analysts, programmers, and technicians at high salaries that would be repaid many times over in savings. Are these supervisors for or against control? Is there a two-party system at work?

There are further vaguenesses in managing salaries. For one thing, unlike hourly wages, salaries are not clearly delineated. Hourly workers are paid a given rate for a given set of job requirements. But salaries are usually expressed in ranges. It's not just the job; it's what the incumbent brings to it. Between the bottom and top of the salary range for any position there may be a spread of as much as 50 percent—depending, supposedly, on the individual's qualifications and performance. How do you budget for such uncertainty, especially in the face of transfers or turnover of incumbents?

And speaking of performance and qualifications, how do you know that individual salaries are really fair? Some supervisors have a way of taking care of deserving candidates. But can you be sure that the money isn't flowing out to yes-men, good talkers, and résumé wavers? You can't help noticing that under new supervision yesterday's high-paid hero has turned into today's high-paid mediocrity—all based on someone's opinion. Have salaries moved up because employees lay emotional blackmail on supervisors who can't say no? Are there sterling employees who are underpaid because they don't speak up for themselves? Have you yourself been conned because you didn't have the support of policies and rules?

From time to time, as if to illuminate these general misgivings, disquieting events occur. A key employee takes off for a better-paying job. A supervisor prefers engaging a new clerk to accepting a higher-salaried internal transferee. Someone turns down a promotion. Total salary increases turn out to be 4 percent more than you budgeted at the beginning of the year. An anonymous letter complains that salary increases have not kept up with the cost of living. An engineer with five years' service remarks that new college graduates are being hired at essentially the same pay as he makes. Despite a no-hiring program, the salary payroll has gone up at a rate faster than that of sales dollars. Analysis discloses that 70 percent of the employees are rated "better than average" on their merit increases—a mathematical anomaly.

Not being an expert in salary matters and wondering if in fact anyone is, the executive ponders a number of questions:

- Are we paying our employees enough?
- Are we paying them too much?
- Are we paying on the same basis in all departments of the company—and do the employees think so?
- Are we attracting and retaining the kind of people we need? Are we losing good employees because of salaries?
- Are we getting motivational power from our salary program—especially from salary increases?
- Is our salary program in control or it is "running free"?
- Are salary procedures taking up too much time?
- Does the salary system encourage or impede promotions and transfers?
- Are our salary costs reliably predictable for budgeting purposes?

These questions may arise in both large and small companies. That the large company can afford a staff of salary specialists does not guarantee that it is free and clear of problems. Often enough, it is locked in an iron cage of assumptions, myths, rules, and procedures that create problems the small company knows not. And by tailoring policies and procedures to fit a vast cosmos of jobs and employees, the large company may end up with a suit that fits no one. The small company, by contrast, has the opportunity to manage its salaries in ways peculiarly appropriate to its own restricted population. But unless it acts on this opportunity, it too will encounter problems.

Smaller establishments can have two big things going for them with respect to salary employees. They can offer to the individual employee an opportunity for freedom, flexibility, creativity, and recognition that is often missing in the castin-concrete corporate monoliths. And in some cases they can afford higher salaries because they are not burdened with the overhead expenses of great corporate superstructures.

These advantages, however, will easily be missed if employees find that the pleasures of a small pond are nullified by capricious or uncertain salary action. Salary measures everything. Nor will the advantages accrue if the employer finds that because of poor salary management, morale is low and, worse yet, overhead costs are high—that too much salary in toto means too little salary to any individual. With good salary management, the employer and the employee know where they stand, and both are relieved of uncertainty.

This book describes briefly methods of salary administration and management that even a smaller employer may use. Its approach is nontechnical. It is designed to be read quickly rather than studied in depth. The emphasis is on salary control. The book focuses on salaries, not total compensation. Incentive bonuses, company-paid insurance and health plans, pensions, and all the other fringes are highly specialized subjects that often require outside consultation. They do not require decisions every day. It is salaries that are in the forefront of employees' minds, and it is salaries that are the bulk of white-collar costs.

The book concentrates on the why and how of salary management. In doing so it looks separately at such salary specifics as structure, ranges, surveys, increases, budgeting, and controls. Throughout the book guidelines and rules will be noted when appropriate, and attention will be directed to problems and risks that may occur.

The book will also describe salary management practices common to large employers, since the small firm must compete with large ones for employees. Through outside contacts its people are often well informed on how their counterparts in large companies are being handled. To keep them satisfied, the smaller employer needs to know the basics of large-firm salary systems in order to adopt good features that suit local requirements while avoiding features that are inappropriate for a more compact organization. As a basic foundation to all these elements the book will also examine the general matter of salary policy.

2: SALARY POLICY

EVERY COMPANY, large or small, has its salary policy, though not necessarily a written one. The policy may consist of detailed rules governing such things as hiring salaries, the amount and timing of salary increases, and payment for jury duty. It may apply rigidly, equally, and without exception to all employees. A more informal policy may consist only of a set of general guidelines that are applied judgmentally in individual cases.

In larger companies, the policy may cover every conceivable salary issue, becoming ultimately more nitty than gritty. In smaller establishments, by contrast, it may address only the major issues of salary, such as an intent to pay at least the going average. In still other companies it may be seemingly nonexistent. No policy is stated. Each employee's compensation is a matter for individual bargaining or decision, as circumstances dictate. But not to have a predetermined policy is itself a policy.

Every firm, then, has some kind of salary policy. This being so, does it really matter whether a company has a conscious, formal, perhaps even written policy or a vague, unformulated one? Let us examine what a formal salary policy may cover.

FORMAL POLICY COVERAGE

Competitive Position. The policy states the establishment's competitive position in the salary field. Is it the firm's intent to pay more than, as much as, or less than the going average for comparable salaried positions?

Salary Levels. The policy defines the nature of salary levels. Is there a salary range? Does everyone doing a given job receive the same pay, or do salaries vary with an employee's competence, years of service, indispensability to the firm, or personal bargaining power?

Salary Determination. The policy defines the means of arriving at salaries or salary ranges for various positions. Are these based simply on surveys of what other companies pay for similar work? Are they arrived at through a job evaluation system? Or are both surveys and job evaluations used?

Salary Increases. The policy defines the basis for salary increases for individuals. Do they occur as a result of inflation, merit, length of service, or a combination of these?

Starting Salaries. The policy defines a means of determining starting salaries for newly hired employees.

Salary Changes. The policy defines what change, if any, occurs in an individual's salary upon promotion, demotion, transfer, or change in duties.

Specials. The policy may cover such related matters—almost procedural—as pay for vacation, holidays, sick leave, time off for funerals, leave of absence, interrupted service, overtime, jury duty, military service, temporary assignments, probationary periods, and advances on pay. These may be set forth in the policy itself or in an appendix of working rules.

SAMPLE POLICY

An example of a written salary policy is presented at the end of this chapter. It is fairly general, referring to guidelines for detail on specific issues. Once an overall, long-term policy has been written, it pays to take the time to set forth the supporting rules for special items, such as those mentioned above. Among other things, such a reference saves argument: "If Schmidt got two days' paid time off for her aunt's funeral in Rochester, why can't I have two days for my cousin's funeral even if it is right here in town?"

Your own policy may not match the sample. In your firm you may wish to be more liberal or more conservative. You may be influenced by factors such as these:

- The terms of your agreement with your hourly workers' union, if any.
- The likelihood that your salaried workers will organize.
- The financial condition of your business.
- The general climate of your establishment. Is it to be Bali Ha'i or the Kremlin?
- The practices in the area, the industry, or competitors' establishments.

If your business is, say, an automobile dealership, you may have too few positions to need the last two sections of the sample (salary changes and specials). On the other hand, if your "small business" is a hospital, with many positions, you may need them.

The sample is illustrative only and cannot be poured directly into any establishment without some adjustment in the ingredients.

ADVANTAGES OF AN UNWRITTEN POLICY

A written policy implies equal treatment of all employees. But salaries are a sensitive issue. Are they not better left to discretion and judgment, and tailoring to the personal situation and contribution of each employee? Is not a salary policy, applying impartially regardless of personal need or contribution, an inhuman straitjacket, the very kind of thing that has spawned the phrase "soulless corporation"?

Perhaps so. As we have seen, some firms have a policy of no policy, or at least no fixed rules except those of judgment: "What seems right, is right." This situation is commonly found in firms so small that one person can handle all salary matters. Say you are the president of an owner-operated company. You know the employees and their abilities. As chief officer you also know how much money can safely be spent on salaries. You hire people and parcel out increases according to an internal knowledge and philosophy that, whether liberal or parsimonious, is probably understood by all. Provided the business can afford it, a cost-of-living and/or merit increase is given every year to everyone at the same time. Or no cost-of-living increase is given, but salary adjustments are made to suit the contribution or even personal circumstances of individuals.

Except that you must always be making decisions, there is nothing much wrong with this policy. In fact, it has some advantages. It can be argued that employees are not entitled to more money just because a calendar date has arrived. They must demonstrate that they deserve more. And if a super employee is worth making happy, a super increase can be given. Why not? Why should one employee be deprived because of arbitrary policies and rules set up to deal with the herd?

ADVANTAGES OF A WRITTEN POLICY

If these are the advantages of an informal, unwritten policy, what are the advantages of one that is spelled out? Why have a written salary policy? For a number of reasons.

Consistency. A written policy ensures consistency, a quality essential to a good working environment. When salary recommendations and decisions are in the hands of a number of supervisors, everybody works under the same rules. If the policy is followed uniformly, one supervisor will not give increases every six months and another every twelve months for the same level of employee performance.

Even in a one-boss shop, the play-to-the-rules discipline of a policy is helpful. It relieves both the boss and the employees of uncertainty. The employees do not have to worry that salary action depends on the boss's mood, whim, favoritism, or memory. The boss does not have to discuss salary matters on the basis of personalities, but can say, more objectively, "That's the policy."

Clarity. A written policy promotes uniform understanding. The basis for determining salary rates for specific jobs and the qualifications for receiving an increase are made known. They are not left to guesswork or to the judgment of different people. This relieves the supervisor of an unnecessary burden.

Cost Control. Adherence to a policy prevents total salary costs from becoming unduly inflated.

Turnover Control. Rational policy guidance means that employees will not leave because of dissatisfaction with capricious salary administration. Nor will they leave because the employer has unwittingly fallen behind the competition.

Career Management. A predetermined scale of salaries appropriate to advancing levels of responsibility or service provides motivation and reward for career advancement.

Continuity. With a written policy, turnover in the supervisory ranks will not disrupt established patterns of salary administration. Even in a one-manager establishment, salary action does not have to come to a standstill, to the distress of employees, if the manager is temporarily replaced.

Fairness. Uniformity, clarity, and continuity of salary administration help to ensure fair and equitable treatment of employees.

Legality. The written statement of, and adherence to, pay practices that apply uniformly is evidence of nondiscrimination. A written policy also provides useful reference data if compensation controls should be imposed.

Simplicity. The firm's salary program can be administered with less confusion and complexity under a predetermined policy than under a system requiring fresh consideration for every salary decision. With a written policy, salary decisions can be delegated rather than always referred to a high-level position.

Predictability. With established rules, future salary costs can be predicted—a boon to budgeting.

These are not only the advantages of a written salary policy. They are also the objectives of a good one. Yet merely having a written salary policy does not guarantee that these advantages will accrue. It is possible to have a policy consisting of empty words.

For example, a statement that "it is the policy of this company that all employees shall be fairly and equitably compensated for work performed" essentially says nothing. In the eyes of some managers, however, it has a certain beauty: by committing the firm to nothing at all, it provides maximum latitude in administering salaries. If it were a firm's basic but unwritten policy to hire employees at the lowest wage possible, to grant increases only to those employees whose departure would be a serious loss, and to withhold increases from employees who are either readily replaceable or highly unlikely to resign—all of which might indeed be a necessary (though unadmirable) approach for an establishment struggling to survive—then such a written policy might be the poor best that could be set forth.

POLICY OBJECTIVES

A good policy is one that has good objectives. It is, moreover, designed in such a way that these objectives can be attained. A good salary policy meets the following criteria:

1. *It is specific.* It defines your firm's competitive position on salaries in relation to the external community in which you compete for employees. It states the internal guidelines for the salaries of positions and of the individuals who fill positions.

2. *It is supported by procedures.* For example, there are rules for determining when, under what circumstances, and in what amount increases shall be given and payments made.

3. *It is flexible.* Room is left for going beyond the rules in exceptional cases.

4. *It is publishable.* The policy is so just that making it known to your employees enhances rather than impairs morale and loyalty to the firm.

This last point can be ticklish. Some firms feel that the less employees know about salary policy the better. If you tell employees too much, they will assume a right to comment on or even to criticize the policy. Why, this puts them in the same position as if they had a union!

On the other hand, behind-the-scenes salary administration is one of the very practices that can encourage a union to form. If you had a union, one of the first things it would do is get into salaries. Then you would have to reveal your policy anyway, and woe to you if it doesn't make sense! So perhaps it is just as well to be open about the matter in advance.

But open about what? This brings us to a final qualification for a good salary policy: you must know what it means.

WHAT DOES THE POLICY MEAN?

If it seems hard to believe that a firm may have a salary policy and yet not know what it means, let us examine a specific case. Suppose your firm has the following policy: "Salaries shall be at least the average of the immediate metropolitan area." Assume you are going to hire a typist who has just graduated from business school. What shall you pay the new employee? Certainly not the average of all typists in the area. Some of them have been on the job for years. This is just a beginning typist. The average of typists' *starting* salaries, then? What starting salaries, in what companies? Does the average include *all* starting salaries—those in small real estate offices as well as those in large corporations?

Perhaps through a survey (we will examine surveys later) you have learned the various starting typists' salaries being offered by other firms in your area. You strike a weighted arithmetic average of these, and this is what you offer. Or you rank the starting salaries from high to low and select the middle one, the median.

Now you know that of the firms hiring typists, half will offer more and half less than you do. At this point a question arises in your mind. If half the firms are able to hire typists for less than the average, why should you pay more than they do? Now you are thinking about what your policy really means.

Let us look at another aspect of this average-pay policy. Suppose you are considering, not starting typists, but people who are already on the payroll—your established workforce.

What does an average-pay policy mean with respect to them?

Let us say that you have eight mechanical engineers on your payroll. Does each of them get the average of the area pay for mechanical engineers? Some of them have been with you for less than two years, and some for more than twenty years. They have varying degrees of ability. So, presumably, do the mechanical engineers working for other companies. When you say that it is your policy to pay at average for the area (or for the industry), an important question arises: Pay whom compared with what?

This again gets us right back to the issue of what the policy means. Clearly, it is desirable to provide some guidance on pay levels. You don't want your firm to shrivel for lack of competent employees; nor do you want it to go bankrupt because of runaway salaries. But before you make general policy statements about pay levels, you should think of their significance in real-world terms. If you tell engineers that you pay average salaries, what does the policy signify in terms of application? Does it mean that any engineer can expect to hit the average? Or does it mean the engineer can expect only the average for people of his or her level of competence or years of experience?

Similarly, if your policy says something about promotional increase, it is a good idea to be clear about what constitutes a promotion. (See Chapter 9.) Again, even though your written policy is general, it should nevertheless be definable.

APPLICATION

A policy has meaning only in its application. If it is to meet certain objectives—fairness, clarity, consistency, and the like—then it must be supported with specific procedures for making it effective. These procedures (or rules or guidelines) spell out just how the policy is put into practice. They may state, among other things:

- The other firms that are to be compared in making salary surveys.
- How salary increases are determined.
- Who must approve salary increases.
- Under what circumstances sick pay is to be granted.
- How overtime pay, if any, is computed.

Generally, policies are expected to provide long-range guidance over the years. They reflect the firm's character and position. The rules and procedures that make them work, however, may go into more detail. Thus, if the *policy* says, "Job for job, we meet the average salaries in our industry," the *rule* may permit increases to average 5 percent in one year and 6 percent in the next—in order to keep up with the industry.

If the *policy* says, "Every employee shall receive at least the minimum of the salary range for the position occupied," the *procedure* may spell out what constitutes occupying a position—that is, how the policy applies to certain circumstances. For example:

- Filling in fully for someone on vacation or sick leave.
- Trying out on a probationary basis.
- Going through a learning period.
- Assuming some, but not all, of the powers of a supervisor who is present but on another assignment.
- Permanent assignment.

If the *policy* says, "The amount of an individual increase shall depend on the quality of job performance," the *guidelines* may tell exactly what percentage increase is given for average performance, what for superior performance, how often, and so on.

Policies, then, declare *what* the firm intends to do. Procedures, rules, and guidelines state *how* the firm will do it.

OBJECTIONS

You may raise some serious objections to all this business of writing out policies and procedures. Too much paperwork. Too many reference manuals. Too much bureaucracy. Too much impersonality. You get enough of this kind of thing from the government!

Still, you can't escape it. You're following *some* kind of policy and procedure, even if it's not in writing.

But why not let it go at that? Why create virtually a Federal Register to record what you know you're doing anyway? There are six reasons why even a small firm should have a written policy (and procedures):

1. It forces you to think through, make sense of, and feel comfortable with what you are doing.

2. It provides reassurance to employees. (Even if they don't see the policy in full detail they know it exists, because they are treated consistently and fairly.)

3. It supplies a controlling mechanism to keep salaried costs in line and to ward off the thrust of individual pressures.

4. It maintains continuity in salary administration. In small firms, and even in larger ones, salary administration is often in the hands of only one person. If this person should be unavailable for some time or should leave the company, the written material enables a successor to take over with a minimum of uncertainty.

5. It stands as a reference and as evidence of a plan in the event of government controls on wages and salaries—or of EEO challenges.

6. It provides useful background for internal audit.

SUBJECT MATTER

With the reminder that policies, guidelines, and procedures sometimes overlap, here are some of the topics they may cover:

Hiring rates
Levels compared with
  other employers
Breadth of salary ranges
Basis for salary increases:
  merit
  tenure
  age
  position in range
  period since last
  percent
  timing
  market advances
  seniority
  general versus individual
Promotions
Demotions
  for cause
  for company purposes
  for personal reasons
Transfers
Red circles
Interruptions in service

Confidentiality
Relation to hourly rates
Overtime
Vacations
Holidays
Leave of absence
Sick pay
Exceptions
Approval levels
Salary advances
Supervisory differentials
Temporary assignments
Separation pay, salary
    continuance, or
   "notice pay"
Probationary pay
Learning pay
Military service
Jury duty
Funeral leave
Temporary hires
Hours of work
School time off

PROBLEMS AND RISKS

There is a certain risk in writing a policy: once you have written it, you are committed to it. Of course, you can just write it for your own guidance and then tuck it away in a drawer. But if it gets out—in fact, if you publicize it in order to reap its undeniable benefits—you are probably going to have to live up to it. Accordingly, it is a good idea to exercise caution in formulating a policy. If there are advantages to having a policy, there are also pitfalls to be avoided. Some of these are discussed below.

Grandiosity. "It is the policy of this firm to pay all employees equitably and fairly for work performed." This sounds great, but does it mean the same thing to you as it does to employees? If, for instance, supervisors read different meanings into it, you should be prepared to live up to it. Let us take an example. In your company the superintendent of the shop grants salary increases on the button when due and in the maximum permissible amount. But the superintendent of warehousing and shipping has trouble with the budget and as a result stretches out review periods and holds increases to the lowest percentage. What purpose does a proclaimed policy of equitable pay serve if two sets of employees are being treated differently?

Overgenerosity. "It is the policy of this firm to pay salaries at least 25 percent more than the average of the industry (or area) for comparable positions." This policy is okay, provided you know what you intend to accomplish by it. Do you expect high pay to attract superior performers? Maybe it will and maybe it won't. It just may attract people who are looking for high pay regardless of their ability. It's your company's recruitment and employment skill, and career opportunities, and stability, and internal environment that determine what kind of people you get. Unless you have something good going in these areas, higher pay won't do it. In fact, if the operations of your firm are confused, whimsical, and uncertain, no amount of pay will hold highly qualified employees. The policy has a noble ring to it. But it can cost a lot of money.

Nonenforcement. "It is the policy of this firm to set a salary range for every position, with the midpoint of the range representing the pay for normal, competent performance of job requirements." You set such a policy and then you, or those under you, fail to follow it. Anyone complaining is told that the policy really can't be interpreted literally or that it doesn't mean what it seems to say. Thus an employee says, "Hey, I was hired only six months ago and I'm doing the same caliber of work as people who've been on my job for ten years. You hired me at the minimum of the range for this job. So now raise me to the midpoint." You say, "Well, no. You have to progress gradually to the midpoint through annual merit increases." How can you expect your employees to buy this distortion of your stated policy and yet be smart enough to work for you?

Exceptions. You have a beautiful set of policies and procedures, but then you violate them. When the supervisor tries to enforce them, people go over his or her head and request an exception. "I know our associate product manager, Wolfe, isn't due for a raise until next December, but if we won't take care of him now, he's going to leave. He's had an offer." So for Wolfe you violate your policy. Two months later he takes that other job anyway, using his higher pay for greater leverage. Before leaving he brags a little to other marketing employees. They find themselves wondering.

Rigidity. A policy so rigidly observed that it leaves no room for appeals or exceptions can do its own kind of damage. Say there is a sudden swell in the demand for spectroscopists, but your policy requires that your own expert fit into the wage curve applicable to all other scientists in the firm. You do not make exceptions to policy, so you lose your spectroscopist. Or say your policy ties the bottom of the salary curve into the top of the hourly wage curve. As a result, you are paying the highest salaries in town for office typists, all for the sake of a rigidly consistent pay curve. It is a *foolish* consistency, let us remember, that Emerson described as a hobgoblin.

Disclosure. In disclosing salary information, there are pitfalls no matter what you do. Let us consider three possibilities.

1. *Total secrecy.* Each employee knows only what his own salary is. He does not know the maximum salary for his position, or the salaries of other positions or employees. He does not know how soon he may expect his next increase, how much it may amount to, or what the amount depends on.

2. *Individual disclosure.* Each employee knows her position in the salary range for her job. She also knows the guidelines that govern review intervals and the varying amounts of increases available (if this is the case) according to position in range, tenure, performance, and so on.

3. *Full disclosure.* Each employee may learn not only the salary status of his or her own job but the salary ranges for other positions, as well as the policies and guidelines governing all aspects of salary administration.

The first alternative, total secrecy, has an advantage. You aren't forced to answer such questions as "When is my next raise?" and "Do I have much future in this job?" This is an advantage, that is, if your workforce is to have a certain uniformity, for it will probably whirl off, like a centrifuge, the more aggressive, independent, career-minded employees and leave you with a thin broth of docile time servers. Employees who grew up in the Great Depression, when jobs were scarce, accept this as the proper way to run a company. They may be right.

Full disclosure, the other extreme, also has its merits. Unlike total secrecy, which suggests that the firm has something to hide, it openly avows the firm's confidence in the fairness of its pay practices. (It may also avow the existence of a union that has demanded disclosure, as a reaction to a previous policy of secrecy.) This approach removes the individual employee's suspicion that others are getting special favors, that the company is trying to hold back on pay, increases, and the like. The pitfall, however, is that it opens the door to amateur job evaluation experts. "Why shouldn't accounts payable clerks make as much as accounts receivable clerks?" "Since when is that job tougher than mine?" "Does this mean that I'm so high in my range I'll *never* get another raise, while a newcomer gets one in six months?"

Perhaps the best solution is individual disclosure, if only because few desirable employees would be satisfied with less. But it has a way of moving beyond itself. Someone offered a promotion or transfer wants to know the range of the proposed job. In time the salary ranges for all jobs spread through the grapevine—with distortions.

No system is perfect. Large institutional organizations that set ranges through remote, hard-to-reach bureaucracies—the government comes to mind—publicize the salaries for all positions and seem to get along. In a smaller organization, with personal pressures, things are not so easy.

SUMMARY

The important thing about salary policy is that it should serve the firm's interests. Salaries are a heavy portion of overhead. Policy helps to keep them in control. It has financial value. In addition, by ensuring consistent treatment to employees, it can have a stabilizing effect on internal relations and contribute to the retention of a career-minded workforce.

Inept policy administration can, on the other hand, create problems. For this reason, the likely effects of salary policies must be carefully considered before the policies are adopted.

XYZ Company Salary Policy

1. RATIONALE: This company is able to compensate adequately only if staffed with employees who contribute to its success through their:
   - Superior ability to perform their jobs.
   - Dedication and interest in performing their jobs.
   - Assistance in helping one another perform their jobs.
2. OBJECTIVE: Salaries shall be such as to attract, retain, and develop employees who have the ability to ensure the company's success (and thereby the success of all its employees).
3. INTERNAL EQUITY OF SALARIES: Salaries shall be internally equitable:
   - An objective system of evaluation shall be used to determine the relative levels of positions; these levels shall be expressed in "salary grades."
   - Each position shall be assigned to a salary grade on the basis of a job description and an evaluation.
   - For every grade, there shall be a "salary range" progressing from a minimum to a maximum.
   - In exceptional cases, to attract scarce skills, a position may be assigned a red-circle range; the evaluation itself shall not deviate from the provisions of the evaluation system.
   - Each regular full-time employee shall be paid at least the mininum of the salary range for the position filled.
4. EXTERNAL COMPETITIVENESS:
   - Salary levels in this company shall be periodically compared with those in the industry and geographic area.

- Salary ranges shall be adjusted as necessary to ensure that they are competitive.
- Employees shall receive individual salary increases to maintain their position in the salary range for the job performed (with the exceptions stated in paragraph 8).

5. INDIVIDUAL MOTIVATION: Salaries shall be individually motivating.
   - Each employee shall be informed of job performance requirements by means of the job description and discussion with the supervisor; each employee shall be given a written copy of the job description and job performance requirements.
   - There shall be a system for supervisory appraisal of individual performance against job requirements.
   - The employee shall participate with the supervisor in such appraisal, shall be informed of its results, and shall be given: (1) a copy of the written appraisal and (2) a written statement of needs or opportunities for performance improvement.
   - Employees shall have periodic opportunities for merit salary increases (progression within range), with an ascending scale of percentage increases depending on quality of performance.
   - All employees shall be informed of opportunities for transfer or promotion through discussion with their supervisor. Nonexempt employees shall also be informed through posting of open positions.

6. TRANSFERS: Employees shall be afforded the opportunity to transfer to positions of the same salary grade in order to broaden their training and/or experience. They may also be requested to transfer to other positions in order to meet company operational needs.

   Lateral Transfers

   Employees transferred from one salaried position to another of the same grade shall receive a prorated salary increase equal to any earned merit increase accumulated to date. The next salary review shall be at the date the original merit review would have occurred without the transfer, and the amount shall equal the remaining prorated portion, based on performance since the date of transfer.

Downward Transfers

- No employee shall be transferred to a position of lower salary grade without the *prior* approval of the president.
- If the downward transfer is due to position elimination or lack of ability to perform the job, the present salary shall be maintained; but no subsequent salary increase shall be given that goes beyond the maximum of the range of the new position.
- If the downward transfer is due to career development or company need for that individual's skills on the new job, a personal red-circle maximum may be established if necessary to permit subsequent merit increases. Such a maximum shall apply only to that individual for tenure in that particular position.
- If the downward transfer is at the employee's request, for personal reasons, the salary of the employee at the new position shall be determined according to the circumstances. This provision includes situations where the employee requests a lower position in lieu of separation or early retirement.
- In no case shall a position be reevaluated to agree with the existing salary grade of a proposed incumbent.

Hourly to Salary Transfers and Promotions

Employees transferred from an hourly paid job to a salaried position shall receive the minimum of the salary range for the position or a salary equal to their current hourly compensation, whichever is greater.

7. PROMOTIONS:

Permanent Promotions

- Every qualified employee who is permanently promoted to a position in a higher grade shall receive, at that time, an increase to at least the minimum salary of the range for the position to which the employee is promoted.
- If the employee's existing salary is already above that

minimum (owing only to overlapping of ranges and not to "red circles"), a promotional increase of X percent shall be given.

- These increases are in addition to the employee's accumulated merit increase, which shall be given at time of promotion.

Temporary Promotions

- Employees who work full time in a position of higher salary grade for a period of one month or more in order to fill in temporarily shall receive an increase to the minimum of the range for the job or X percent, whichever is greater, for each full half-month worked. Upon return to the former lower-grade position, the employee shall receive a salary equal to the amount paid prior to the temporary promotion, plus any merit increase falling due during this period.

8. REEVALUATIONS: Each time a job description is revised, the position shall be reevaluated to ensure the maintenance of internal comparative relationships.

Upgrading

- Employees in positions that have been upgraded as a result of reevaluation shall receive at least the minimum of the range of the new salary grade.
- In no case shall a position be upgraded solely to provide a "promotion" for a present or proposed incumbent.

Same Grade

- Employees in reevaluated positions that have not changed salary grades shall have no salary adjustment at the time; rather, normal merit reviews shall continue under the regular program.

Downgrading

- Employees in positions that have been downgraded as a result of reevaluation shall have no adjustment in salary; rather, future merit reviews shall be based on the new (lower) salary grade and the Salary Increase Guide.

9. SEPARATION OR TERMINATION:

Voluntary Resignations

- Voluntary resignation by an employee shall result in settlement of all payments and adjustments due through the last day worked. Settlement equals salary plus accumulated vacation pay, less advances on salary and expenses due the company.

Involuntary Separations

- Terminations (discharge), with proper approvals, for violation of company rules and regulations, neglect of work, or insubordination shall result in settlement of all payments and adjustments due through the last day worked.

- Separations, with proper approvals, due to the employee's lack of ability to perform, reduction in the workforce, or discontinuance or removal of company operations shall entitle employees to a separation allowance in addition to settlement of all payments and adjustments due. The allowance shall equal one week's pay for each full year of service.

- In the event of an employee's death, salary and vacation pay due shall be paid through the last day of the month in which the death occurs.

10. DISCLOSURE: In order that the salary policy may achieve its purpose of attracting, retaining, developing, and motivating high-performance employees, each salaried employee shall be provided with:

- Job description and job performance requirements.
- Salary grade of the position.
- Salary range corresponding to that grade.
- Salary Increase Guide of percentage increases and intervals corresponding to various levels of performance.

3: JOB EVALUATION

IN MOST COMPANIES the salary of an employee depends, at least in part, on the nature of the job performed. The file clerk gets one level of salary, the tool room foreman gets another. By how much should the tool room foreman's salary differ from the file clerk's? This is one of the issues that salary management must deal with.

If only one or two jobs are involved, the matter can easily be settled by finding out what other companies pay. But if there are scores of positions, it is impossible to relate each directly to those in other companies. Some positions may, in fact, have no exact counterpart elsewhere. What you must do is work out the internal architecture of the job structure. This is most commonly done through job evaluation (JE).

The purpose of job evaluation is to determine the relationship among the various salaried jobs, or positions, in the company. Not among the people, but among the positions they fill.

We should be clear as to what is meant by "relationship." The term refers to the relationship between the salary levels of the various jobs. It is hard to imagine bothering with job evaluation except to determine the relative pay levels of jobs.

Generally, a JE system attempts to measure this relationship in terms of what is required for job performance. The greater the skills needed, the greater the complexity of the job, the heavier the requirements for motivating people, and the weightier the effect on controllable costs, then the higher the evaluation will be. If the basic measures of the system are correct, the higher and lower evaluations will at least roughly correspond to higher and lower salaries for the various jobs in the marketplace.

At the same time, there are some things that evaluation does not measure. It does not measure the worth or value to the company of any job—except in terms of what the company is willing to pay for it. The gate guard may be "worth" several million dollars to a company if he stops a terrorist on the way in with an attaché case—but this does not mean he should be paid more than the CEO. Nor does job evaluation assign degrees of importance or difficulty to jobs. For example, one of the most difficult jobs in the company may be taking dictation from old Mr. Brandywine and then trying to figure out what he meant. But this does not call for a high evaluation. Similarly, the boiler room superintendent may declare, "My job is the most important. Without it the whole plant shuts down." Or someone may say, "The salesman's job is of the greatest value to the firm." It is easy to see why job evaluation should avoid terms like "worth," "value," "importance," and "difficulty."

JOB DESCRIPTIONS

The first step in job evaluation is to obtain a job description. Descriptions can be written by (1) a job analyst, (2) the incumbent in the job, or (3) the supervisor of the job.

The first approach is to have an analyst write job descriptions. In this case, the descriptions will contain at least the *kinds* of information needed for evaluation. Also, they will be uniform in style. Since, however, few analysts are apt to know the content of every job, interviewing is required. This ties up at least two people: the interviewer and the interviewee.

The second approach is to let the incumbent fill out a job description questionnaire. The questions should be designed to elicit specific job information: How many people do you directly supervise? What duties do you perform? What kinds of things do you have to know? What decisions do you make on your own? On what basis? What outside people do you contact? Reviewing these questionnaires requires careful judgment, since responses will vary widely. Some may be terse and uninformative. Others may be a little, let us say, overblown. For example, the stock records clerk may give an impression of being solely in control of the expenditure of several hundred thousand dollars.

If there are a dozen different incumbents in the same position, twelve descriptions must be reviewed—not wholly a bad thing for the varying facets revealed, and certainly better than interviewing twelve people. Incumbents' descriptions should, of course, be reviewed and approved by the supervisor.

The third approach is to let the supervisor write the description (also by means of a questionnaire, if desired). The advantage here is that the supervisor will describe what is expected of the job, which may go a little beyond what the incumbent thinks is expected and thus serve a training purpose. A possible disadvantage is that busy supervisors who oversee a multitude of jobs don't always have time to write out job descriptions.

Uses of Job Descriptions

Job descriptions have two immediate purposes. First, they provide information for use in evaluating jobs. Second, they serve as a record in case a job subsequently requires reevaluation—because of either a change in duties or a doubt about the original evaluation's validity.

Other possible uses for job descriptions include:

1. Giving them to employment agencies and recruiters when a vacancy is to be filled.
2. Using them as educational devices for employees new to a job.
3. Using them to set performance objectives.
4. Basing performance appraisals on their requirements.
5. Referring to them for outlining career paths.
6. Giving them to employees who wish to learn about a job they are considering for transfer or promotion.
7. Using them for systems studies and methods improvements.
8. Giving them to newly appointed supervisors so they can learn about their areas of management.
9. Basing disciplinary measures for nonfeasance on their requirements.
10. Supplying them to respondents in compensation surveys.
11. Determining areas of need or interest for training programs.
12. Consulting them to be sure that someone is clearly accountable for everything that needs to be done in the company. (For example, what position is responsible for periodic tests of the sprinkler system? What position is responsible for seeing that internal new developments are protected with patents?)
13. Forecasting future skills requirements from them, in long-range human resources planning.
14. Using them to fit together responsibilities in restructuring the firm's organization.

Sometimes, in connection with items 13 and 14, descriptions are written for positions that may not come into existence until some time in the future.

In contrast to these many uses, some people find non-uses

for job descriptions. In Japanese companies, we are told, "Traditional job descriptions are deemphasized. Without such descriptions, supervisors are encouraged to be flexible, to accept more responsibility."[*] To us, this approach may seem a little self-defeating. If you want a supervisor to "accept" more responsibility, why not say so and put it in the job description?

Job Description Content

What goes into the description is what is needed for the uses described above. Title, job number, department, date— of course. One or two introductory sentences on the general purpose of the position—preferably a brief description of why the job exists and what it is expected to accomplish.

Beyond this, the description should supply information that relates to the characteristics being evaluated. If budget responsibility is a factor, then the budgeted dollars should be stated. If outside contacts have a bearing, they should be named.

Language should be specific and precise. An analyst evaluating a job from its description will have trouble with a statement like "maintain repair parts inventory." Does this mean safeguard the inventory in the stockroom, post it on ledger accounts or stock cards, order replenishments, or perform physical repairs on parts? These are quite different activities, all inferable from the word "maintain," and could lead to different evaluations.

The descriptions should provide sufficient detail to disclose the scope of the job. "Operate gas chromatograph" is not enough. Using the instrument day in and day out on repeated tests of a single substance is not at all the same as being able to analyze any unknown on it.

---

[*] *Board Room Reports,* May 15, 1978, p. 3.

What the description should do, in short, is give the evaluator something to evaluate. Consider this excerpt from a job description for the position "sales representative":

A. *Sells and promotes the sale of all company products:*
   1. Obtains maximum distribution of all authorized varieties.
   2. Sells new sizes and products to obtain distribution objectives in all stores.
   3. Installs and maintains departments to meet or exceed objectives.
      - Sells such programs to each store manager as the means for increasing total sales or eliminating out-of-stock situations.
      - Works continually to improve shelf space and position of varieties.
   4. Executes promotional campaigns to result in features and displays.
      - Secures such displays on the basis of national and local promotional objectives, opportunities identified within the store, and the size and merchandising potential of individual stores.
      - Ensures that all promotions sold are executed effectively in all stores in compliance with headquarters-approved promotions.

RANKING

Evaluation leads to a ranking of jobs, top to bottom. Ranking provides a means of relating jobs to rates of pay. As long as the jobs remain unchanged, the ranking is permanent. But as market pay scales change, different salaries can from year to year be laid against the ranked jobs. Thus three jobs might line up as follows:

	Monthly Salary		
Title	*Year 1*	*Year 2*	*Year 3*
Secretary A	$800	$850	$900
Secretary B	700	740	785
Secretary C	600	635	675

The question is: How is the ranking arrived at?

Position Ranking

One simple approach is to consider the promotional relationship among the positions. For example, the ranking ladder in a factory might be as follows:

Factory manager
General superintendent
Department head
Supervisor

This succession does not, however, tell you how much "space" there should be between positions. You could estimate this distance judgmentally. For example, you could say that the department head should receive at least 15 percent more than the supervisor. Or you could survey other companies to see how the pay of similar positions relates. Either way, you could set up a scale of pay ratios:

Position	*Ratio*
Factory manager	3.00
General suprintendent	2.00
Department head	1.15
Supervisor	1.00

Thus, if the supervisor's base pay is $1,000 a month, the department head's is $1,150. These ratios can be maintained even if inflation requires upward adjustments in dollar values from year to year. (Note that these are *base* salaries. As described in Chapter 4, each base salary may be surrounded by a range to take care of differences in the personal qualifications of incumbents.)

But this does not say anything about other related positions. The factory has a manager of factory accounting. Perhaps you would place this position below the general superintendent but above the department head—say, at 1.50. It has a manager of quality control, a position above department head, possibly one from which you would promote to general superintendent and one that has greater technical qualifications than the accounting manager. It could fall at, say, 1.75.

Such a system is simple and can work well. In a small owner-operated company, it can be handled by the president alone. In a larger company, a committee of people familiar with all activities can fit jobs into rankings, using their judgment and perhaps some survey data on pay relationships.

Ranking systems of this sort have a long history. Here, for example, is a very similar arrangement described by Mencius,* a Confucian philosopher who lived around 300 B.C.:

> In a great State . . . the sovereign had ten times as much income as the chief ministers; a chief minister four times as much as a great officer; a great officer twice as much as a scholar of the first class; a scholar of the first class twice as much as one of the middle; a scholar of the middle class twice as much as one of the lowest. The scholars of the lowest class, and such of the common people as were employed about the government offices, had the same emolument—as much, namely, as was equal to what they would have made by tilling the fields.

* *The Works of Mencius,* Book V, Part II, Chapter 2, verse 6.

Thus position ranking can be grouped with gunpowder and spaghetti as one of those ornaments of civilization invented by the Chinese.

Success in Ranking

A difficulty of ranking systems is their weakness in the face of challenge. Suppose the department head in our example says, "I notice that my salary level is only 15 percent above the supervisor's. I think 20 percent would be fairer." How is this to be answered? By saying, "Well, in my judgment . . ."? The point is the department head is questioning your judgment. How do you support your judgment?

One way is to discuss some of the characteristics of the job. It requires, you say, no more technical knowledge than the supervisor's. But it does need more knowledge of human relations. And it has a larger budget to control. But the amount of actual control is minimal, since costs are pretty well determined by union contracts and production schedules. The complexity is greater: the department head has to solve problems that the supervisor doesn't. And the department head has to make more decisions—he or she is, in fact, the person to whom the supervisor takes the tough ones. The supervisor works from day to day, but the department head has to plan a week in advance. Still, longer-range planning is handled by the general superintendent, so the department head's requirements in this area are fairly limited.

Now you have mentioned a number of characteristics: education, experience, controllable spending, complexity, decision making, planning. But what weight did you give to them? And how did consideration of these lead to the 15 percent (rather than 20 percent) differential? In a simple ranking scheme, the only answer is judgment. Judgment did it. Rational, not capricious, judgment.

How well this answer can stand up depends on how people

feel about the source of the judgment. If there is a general atmosphere of trust, they will be satisfied that the judgment is good, or at least supportable. And this statement can be reversed. If the ranking of jobs makes sense to people, an atmosphere of trust will be encouraged.

Ranking systems can work well if:

1. There are promotional relationships among jobs.
2. Pay levels, job for job, compare favorably with those elsewhere.
3. Ranking is performed by people familiar with the positions and their requirements.
4. Ranking is performed impersonally and objectively.
5. Ranking is performed by people whose judgment is respected.
6. The general atmosphere is one of trust and acceptance rather than antagonism.
7. The number of positions in the company is fairly small—say, fewer than 100.

Advantages of Ranking Systems

Although position ranking systems may seem unsophisticated, they do have certain advantages. To begin with, the rankings can be based on job descriptions, which become a matter of record, for reference. In addition, the rankings can be done by a person or committee having fairly complete knowledge of job relationships. Also, the reasons for each job ranking can be made a matter of record, again for future reference in case of challenge or change. For example, the rankings may have been compared with survey data for comparable jobs, which can be recorded.

The system can be sufficiently flexible to accommodate conditions peculiar to the company. For example, it can recognize those situations where a job is really shaped by the individual who fills it. Such a position would be ranked differently from what it might be with another incumbent.

There is nothing inherently wrong with simple ranking systems if they are managed properly. Still, many companies have found that it is a natural step to go from simple systems to more formalized factor-point systems.

JOB FACTORS

As we have seen, in ranking jobs it is frequently necessary to consider which characteristics of the jobs determine the pay relationships. What is it about some jobs, other than mere hierarchical position on the organization chart, that makes them "fuller" than others—that enables them to command more pay than others?

There are several determining influences. For example, the performance of a job may call for a great deal of know-how. Presumably, relatively few people have this background. We will have to pay more for these people in order to get and hold on to them. If a job demands a great deal of mental acuity, judgment, or foresight, our knowledge of bell curves tells us that relatively few people have a lot of these attributes. Again we will have to pay more.

If a job involves great complexity or risk of failure, relatively few competent people will wish to expose themselves to it. We will have to pay more to entice them to take it. If a job requires great ability to manage and motivate other people, those who have this ability will be in great demand. We will have to pay more for them.

What we are talking about here are job factors: knowledge, mental skill, judgment, decision making, and the like. In fact, we are talking about *compensable* factors. Someone says, "I deal with customers, so I have to be neatly dressed. Isn't appearance a factor?" Well, yes, it may be, but it's not a compensable factor. The job doesn't pay more because of it.

Suppose you were to make a list of the compensable factors common to most jobs in your company. In considering any job, you could ask yourself, "How much of each factor does it require?" To get a handle on the "how much," you could assign a scale of point values to each factor. Then "how much" would mean "how many points."

In this way you would approach having a numerical measure for each job. This measure would be determined by an examination of the job's characteristics as reported in the job description. The more of a characteristic a job demands, the greater the measure. The results would be internally consistent, since all jobs are compared against the same uniform set of measures.

What are the factors that vary from job to job? Many lists of such factors have been devised. Some are found in job evaluation systems available from consultants or trade associations. Others have been developed internally by companies for their own use. Some have been identified by industrial psychologists. Some factors that distinguish among jobs are the "traits" listed in the *U.S. Government Dictionary of Occupational Titles.*

Here are examples of some of the factors that can be used to determine differences among jobs:

Depth of knowledge

Education or training

Scope of management

Freedom to think

Freedom to act

Number of people supervised

Human relations skills required

Outside contacts required

Controllable expense dollars managed

Value of assets controlled

Risk of exposure

Peer contacts

Degree of authority

Extent of responsibility

Decision making
Variety
Manual skills
Creativity or ingenuity
Effort
Accountability for end
  results
Planning horizon
Complexity

Amount of supervision
  received
Extent to which work is
  checked or reviewed
Safety hazards
Physical working conditions
Organizational level
Length of experience
Problem solving

Most evaluation systems employ a limited number of these factors.

FACTOR-POINT SYSTEMS

A factor-point system for evaluating salaried positions has the following features:

1. It identifies a set of factors that are present in varying degrees in most of the jobs under study.
2. For each factor, it provides a scale of point values.
3. For each factor, it provides a series of defining statements associated with each level, or degree, of point values.
4. For any job, the "amount" of each factor present can thus be stated in terms of points.
5. The sum of the points from all the factors is the point value of the job.

To illustrate, let us assume a very simple evaluation plan. It has four factors:

Knowledge
1. Elementary knowledge: simple arithmetic, reading, punctuation   10 points
2. English grammar, typing, laboratory and/or clerical procedures, departmental systems   20 points

   3. Companywide systems, applied technologies   30 points
   4. Nonprofessional skills   40 points
   5. Professional skills   50 points
   6. Advanced professional skills   60 points

Initiative
1. Follow detailed instructions or procedures in repetitive situations   10 points
2. Follow detailed instructions in varied situations   20 points
3. Select established method of doing specific tasks to achieve specified end results   30 points
4. Develop method for achieving specified end results   40 points
5. Determine end results to be achieved in own job or in jobs supervised   50 points
6. Determine policies   60 points

Complexity
1. Perform essentially same functions daily   10 points
2. Perform variety of functions that repeat weekly or monthly   20 points
3. Perform variety of unrepetitive functions   30 points
4. Integrate related functions   40 points
5. Integrate conflicting functions   50 points

Supervision
0. Supervise no one   0 points
1. Act as lead person in small group   10 points
2. Supervise up to 10 people   20 points
3. Supervise 11 to 30 people   30 points
4. Supervise 31 to 100 people   40 points
5. Supervise 101 to 500 people   50 points
6. Supervise over 500 people   60 points

Under this very sketchy plan, you might evaluate the typist job as follows:

Knowledge	level 2	20 points
Initiative	level 1	10
Complexity	level 1	10
Supervision	level 0	0
	Total	40 points

The first-line factory supervisor might get:

Knowledge	level 2	20 points
Initiative	level 3	30
Complexity	level 4	40
Supervision	level 3	30
	Total	120 points

The factory manager might get:

Knowledge	level 5	50 points
Initiative	level 5	50
Complexity	level 5	50
Supervision	level 6	60
	Total	210 points

The head of a small research lab, performing assignments under presidential direction, might get:

Knowledge	level 6	60 points
Initiative	level 4	40
Complexity	level 4	40
Supervision	level 2	20
	Total	160 points

Thus, by matching each job to the appropriate level of each factor, you have determined a total point value for it. In each case you have evaluated the job itself, not the person filling it. And you have evaluated in terms of average, not ideal, requirements.

A ranking of the jobs according to points would show:

Factory manager	210 points
Research head	160 points
Factory supervisor	120 points
Typist	40 points

Using factor-point values provides not only a top-to-bottom ranking of the jobs but also the amount of "space" between job levels, something that simple judgmental ranking, un-aided by a system, cannot do.

Once point values are arrived at for all jobs in the com-pany, the scale of points can be related to a salary curve. That is, job salary levels can be set for corresponding point levels. As a very simple example, you could have a point-to-salary conversion formula in which for any job:

Monthly salary = $280 + ($13 × number of points)

Then the typist job (40 points) would have a monthly salary of $280 + ($13 × 40) = $800. The factory manager job would have a monthly salary of $280 + ($13 × 210) = $3,010.

Under such an arrangement, the point level for a job is per-manent until the job itself changes in its requirements. Salary values per point may, however, be adjusted from time to time to keep pace with changes in the economy. In fact, a job list-ing, with point values, can be fed into the company com-puter, along with the point-to-salary conversion formula. If the formula is changed to reflect new salary levels in the job market, the computer can issue a new salary tabulation. (Sal-ary curves are discussed more fully in Chapter 4.)

JE point systems are not a science. They are a device in-tended to focus and quantify comparisons. A properly con-structed system has the following characteristics:

1. It establishes factors that cut across most of the jobs in the organization.
2. It establishes arbitrary levels representing various degrees of each factor.
3. It defines each level in language such that different people, familiar with the system, can arrive at identical evaluations for a given job.
4. It provides a sufficient number of levels to cover the range of jobs in the company and to distinguish between jobs that an informed, reasonable person could see falling in different scalar rankings.

CROSS-CHECKING

Few jobs exist in isolation. They are related in some way to other jobs. Thus a good evaluation system does more than merely work out the points for a job as though that job were freestanding. It also cross-checks the results with the points for jobs that are in some way comparable to the one in question. For example, if you are evaluating the job "shipping clerk," you would compare the results with the points already assigned to the similar position "receiving clerk." You would also check against the points for the next job up the promotional ladder (head shipper, perhaps). If the clerk comes out higher, you have a problem.

Cross-checking should be done not only by total points but, better yet, factor by factor. For example, how do the Knowledge points for shipping clerk compare with those for other jobs?

BENCHMARKS

"Benchmark" jobs are a useful adjunct to either point or straight ranking systems. The benchmark list is a set of jobs used for reference purposes. Usually these are positions that:

- Typify various pay levels throughout the company.
- Represent various departments and job families (clerical, engineering, manufacturing, selling, and the like) throughout the company.
- Are considered to be fairly paid in comparison with one another.
- Exist in other companies as well, to serve as a basis for salary survey comparisons.

When a job has been evaluated, by any method, the result can be compared with the benchmark list to see if it "fits" well with others that have previously been evaluated.

PROBLEMS AND RISKS

As noted earlier, the evaluation plan illustrated here is a simplified one. It has its deficiencies, and so in fact do some of the more elaborate plans in use. Two kinds of problems may arise: problems of design and problems of application.

Problems of Design

When the design of a plan does not fit the conditions of its use, problems will arise. Thus an evaluation scheme devised specifically for an insurance company may not be readily applicable to, say, a motion-picture business. The factors would not mesh with all the jobs. Not all plans, however, are so narrowly defined. Many are intended to be applicable to any salaried position anywhere, from mail clerk to president of a conglomerate. Even with them, difficulties may occur.

Missing Factors. The plan may not recognize differences that people in your organization consider when they compare jobs. For example, our illustrative plan has only four factors. Surely other factors also influence the salaried ranking of positions. For example, some form of creativity must be an ingredient in the upper levels of copywriting, machine design, product formulation, and industrial engineering. Yet our plan does not include creativity, or even problem solving, as a factor.

Any plan that omits truly distinguishing factors will probably fail to measure the differences among jobs that the jobholders themselves will sense.

Improper Weighting. Arbitrary factor weighting can cause problems. The weights assigned to the factors should realistically reflect the influence of the factors on job relationships. In our example, Supervision and Knowledge have the same range of point values. As a result, the head of the research lab gets only a few more points than a first-line supervisor. But this may not represent the real-life relationship between the positions—especially in terms of going salaries, which job evaluation is supposed to reflect. Distorted point values in the basic plan can unduly suppress or elevate whole groups of jobs—leading to "evaluated" relationships among, say, technological, accounting, manufacturing, and marketing positions that do not reflect the community facts of life.

Insufficient Range. In our example, there are six levels of Supervision (excluding level 0—"supervise no one"). This may not provide enough scope in organizations that have, say, eight levels of supervision from top to bottom. Similarly, the levels of Knowledge may not be sufficient to discriminate among existing jobs—for example, between a typist and an executive secretary. The plan squeezes together jobs that are in fact graded in successively higher ranges. As a result, the position points derived will not provide promotional distinctions.

Overprecision. Factor language that is too precise leads to artificial jumps in job point values. In our example, supervision of 11 to 30 people is worth 30 points and 31 to 100 people, 40 points. This makes sense in a general way: the more people supervised, the tougher the job. At the same time, it makes no sense at all to say that supervising 31 people is worth 10 full points more than supervising 30. As a matter of fact, the average supervisor, if aware of the rules of the plan, would have a good incentive not to cut costs but to enlarge his or her empire by one person. A JE system that defines levels too rigidly produces hard-to-buy evaluations.

Overgenerality. By contrast, factor levels that are defined in overgeneral terms are hard to use consistently. Suppose, for example, that we have a factor called Complexity, with its levels defined as follows:

Complexity
1.	Little or no complexity	10 points
2.	Normal complexity	20 points
3.	Moderately heavy complexity	30 points
4.	Fairly heavy complexity	40 points
5.	High complexity	50 points

There isn't much here to guide evaluators. They read a job description and, on their own interpretation of such words as "moderately" or "fairly" heavy, assign points to the job. Perhaps they rely on recollection or on a listing of how other jobs have been interpreted.

If only one person were doing the evaluating, there would at least be a chance for consistency. But suppose a new evaluator appears, to whom "moderately" has a different connotation. Worse, suppose a union steward enters the picture and challenges an evaluation: "I say this job involves 'heavy complexity,' not 'moderate'!" What does the evaluation system provide to resolve the argument? Vague and imprecise language raises at least as many problems as excessively definitive wording.

Unvalidated Factors. Some older job evaluation systems include factors that sound reasonable but aren't. For example, suppose you include Education and Experience as two of your compensable factors. Jobs requiring a high degree of education and experience would then pay more than those that get along with less. The various levels of each factor might be as follows:

Education
1. Grade school   10 points
2. Two years of high school   15 points
3. High school   20 points
4. Some college   25 points
5. Bachelor of arts degree   30 points
6. Bachelor of science degree   35 points
7. Master's degree   40 points
8. Ph.D. or equivalent   50 points

Experience
1. None   0 points
2. 1–3 months   5 points
3. 3–6 months   10 points
4. 6–12 months   15 points
5. 1–2 years   20 points
6. 2–5 years   25 points
7. Over 5 years   30 points

The difficulty arises in trying to apply these factors to specific jobs. For example, you may decide that a computer operator needs "some college—25 points." But then it occurs to you that there are kids running computers in high school. Do the history, economics, and English literature that students get in their first two years of college really have anything to do with running a computer? You then back off to "high school—20 points." But again, might not someone get through high school and have learned nothing of relevance to computer operation? The factor is difficult to tie in to the job.

"Experience" poses similar difficulties. How do you measure its effects? Suppose you decide that an average employee should have three years of experience to qualify as a supervisor. What kind of experience? If someone argued that five years were required, what facts would you cite to justify your position? Once again, the factor is easy to grasp intuitively but hard to apply in a defensible way.

In both cases, it is better to use factors that evaluate those job characteristics that draw on education or experience. Thus the factors "Knowledge" and "Complexity" in the preceding sample evaluation plan address what must be done on the job rather than the amount of preparation to do it. With this approach you evaluate the job, not the qualifications of the incumbent.

Problems of Application

However well a plan is designed, it may still encounter problems in its application. These may be due either to some failing on the part of those doing the evaluating or to pressures put on the evaluators by others in the organization. The first type of problem arises from inadequate rules and training. The second arises from the fact that people are people.

Various problems of application are examined below.

Bias. The person performing the evaluation may be subconsciously biased on some jobs. This can work in either of two ways. Say your evaluator has had previous experience in the accounting department. The work of accountants is familiar. The work of chemists, on the other hand, is terra incognita. When the evaluator reads an accounting job description, it looks routine and "open." A chemist's job description looks difficult and mysterious. The evaluator tends to evaluate accounting jobs a little too low and chemists' jobs a little too high.

Another person, in the same circumstances, may come up with an opposite bias. This evaluator is loyal to accountancy. It is a worthy and demanding profession. The evaluator subconsciously rates accounting jobs relatively higher than those in other fields.

Title Evaluation. Evaluating the title rather than the job is an easy trap to fall into. Evaluators should be guided by what the job description says, not what the job is called. Often enough titles, informally assigned in the past, can be misleading. Consider a job called "office clerk." "Clerk" sounds like a job that would evaluate low. But suppose that this "clerk" is in fact responsible for all credit checks, decisions on limits of credit, assignment of debts to collection agencies, and acceptance or rejection of orders. The position may, despite its title, be a highly responsible one, deserving higher ranking than that of a mere copier of numbers. On the other hand, suppose that the person who writes up orders has been dubbed "general manager–sales" just to provide a little prestige in dealing with customers. The fancy title need not influence the evaluation. What the person does, not what the job is called, is what counts.

Vague Descriptions. The evaluator may simply have trouble understanding the job. Does or does not this manager of quality assurance have a veto power on design? Can the quality manager shut down a production line, and if so does this mean that the incumbent has greater decision-making power than the plant manager? The evaluator, if a skeptic, may get the right answers by asking questions. Acceptance of the first glib answers, however, may lead to evaluation of a job that doesn't exist.

Vague Structure. The allocation of accountabilities in the organization may be so vague that it is difficult to pin down who is ultimately answerable for what. Thus the quality assurance manager may have veto power in some circumstances and not in others. The extent of authority may depend on what kind of person the incumbent is. The position, as an abstraction, is difficult to define.

Sometimes the problem lies in the organization structure. People trade on and off jobs and fill in for each other. More than one person may be handing out instruction and supervision in a given department. This situation is not uncommon in small companies. But it may occur in large ones as well, especially those with a matrix organization. Everybody is in charge, so every job rates high. Relatively high point values are assigned to many jobs rather than concentrated in a few.

Seasonality. Jobs that change throughout the year present evaluation problems. For example, in some businesses seasonality affects job demands. Thus in a small food business a position may, for many months of the year, require only routine, low-level skills. Then for one or two months the business goes into high gear, conflicts multiply, and the position puts super pressures on the incumbent. Should this position receive high points for the peak period requirements? This is the "brain surgeon" situation: if you want someone who can do neurosurgery on demand, you will have to pay for that skill, even though most of the time the physician may be pasting bandages on cut fingers.

Exaggeration. Supervisors or employees, in an effort to upgrade a job, sometimes exaggerate its requirements. Often they do this with an imposing job description which magnifies every possible duty in order to suggest labyrinthine complexity. Sometimes they do it by attributing to a low-level position a decision-making power that really resides in its superior, or by confusing routine functions (such as *processing* budgets and inventory records) with managerial ones (such as *determining* budgets and inventory levels). Another form of exaggeration is to stipulate knowledge or educational requirements that are not really employed in the duties performed. For example, an employee states expansively that a college education is required for the position of buyer (after which the incumbent is transferred and his or her undegreed secretary, thoroughly familiar with the job, is moved into it). The question in all these cases is: What are the true basic duties of the job?

EEO Risks. As a corollary to the preceding example, stipulating job qualifications not consistent with duties may be a form of discrimination. It may introduce artificial barriers that deny people admittance to lower-paying entry-level jobs. Such a practice may reflect past promotional patterns—for example, hiring college graduates as bank tellers, not because the teller's job itself requires a college degree but because the position is a training ground and reservoir for higher positions that do. The same thing may happen with lower-level clerical, technical, and supervisory positions. High entrance requirements may discriminate against candidates who, though capable of performing the jobs in question, do not have the advantage of higher education. "Jacks or better to open" keeps people out of the game.

If reflected in the evaluation, such requirements also result in unnecessarily high point values, to the company's cost. This creates a real dilemma for companies that want to break in college graduates on jobs that do not pay graduates' starting salaries. But this is a pay problem, not one to be solved by overevaluating training positions.

Even when simple ranking is used, without point evaluation, bias may creep in. A good test: Would I rank this job in the same way if it were filled by someone of a different age, race, or sex?[*]

Ad Hoc Pressures. Occasionally there are attempts to "bend" evaluation to a secondary purpose. For example, a supervisor may have a problem with an individual employee's salary, for one of the following reasons:

- Employee is due for an increase but is at the top of the salary range for the position as it is evaluated.
- Employee has an offer of a better job and can supposedly be retained only by upping the salary range (and salary) on the job now occupied.
- Employee is desired for transfer into the job in question but is already making a salary higher than evaluation supports for the job.
- Employee has asked for a promotion, but no openings exist; therefore, the supervisor wants to retitle the pres-

---

[*] Increasingly, job evaluation systems are being cited as examples of discrimination in action. An excellent summary of the problem is presented in David J. Thomsen, "Eliminating Pay Discrimination Caused by Job Evaluation," *Personnel*, September–October 1978.

ent job, upgrade it, and give employee a promotional increase.

In all these cases there is pressure to assign more points to the job in order to solve a salary problem. This distorts the point relationship with other jobs.

New Jobs. When new departments are created or new systems are installed, new jobs occur. During the start-up period, exceptional abilities are required for devising new methods and debugging. After a time, things settle into a routine. The evaluator may be under considerable pressure to analyze the jobs on their going-in demands. Later on these evaluations, unless corrected downward (always difficult to do), will seem high compared with other jobs in the company.

Changed Jobs. From time to time, duties are added to or taken away from existing positions. Without fail, the evaluator will be asked if the added duties do not justify a higher point rating. ("You can't expect people to take on additional responsibility without giving them something in return!") Less often will the evaluator be asked to make a downward evaluation following removal of duties from a position. In both cases the job *should* be reevaluated. But this evaluation should not be in terms of points added to or deducted from the activities in question. Rather, a completely new evaluation should be performed for the job, just as if it were a new job. The changed duties may or may not have altered the point status of the job.

EVALUATION SPECIALISTS

Evaluation may be performed by JE specialists. Often they are part of the personnel department. At first blush, merging job evaluation with salary administration seems like a natural blend. After all, the two functions are closely related. One determines job levels; the other handles job pay. This teaming up is not uncommon, but it is far from ideal. A better arrangement is to separate the two.

Job evaluation is concerned with internal relations among positions. Its objective is to quantify the requirements of each job in comparison with others. It is blind to people. It should not be primarily concerned with or influenced by the rates of pay of individuals.

Salary administration, on the other hand, is concerned with dollars and with people. Since these are touchy subjects, salary administration frequently runs into problems, usually of the kind where an adjustment is desired in a person's salary. One tempting way to adjust salary is to change the evaluation. Doing so solves the immediate issue. However, it also warps the objectively assessed relationship among jobs. Further, evaluation of future jobs will be more difficult when an attempt is made to fit them into the new, inconsistent ranking. If salary is the problem, reevaluation should not be the easy solution.

Separating job evaluation from salary administration supports the integrity of both. It also provides useful checks and balances.

Even when set up as an independent function, evaluation by specialists has its disadvantages. The evaluators are at one remove from other departments and thus may not fully understand all jobs. They are at the mercy of the job descriptions, which may or may not be complete. They have to rely on what people tell them. As a result, they may misevaluate.

Moreover, confining the JE machinery to one area gives a "black box" quality to the process, which may impair confidence in it. Most troublesome of all, supervisors dissatisfied with an evaluation—or with the salary range stemming from it—can go over an evaluator's head with a request for a change. This is especially likely if they outrank the evaluator. Then a decision will be made by an executive anxious to smoothe ruffled feathers. The executive won't be heavily influenced by what seem to be the nitpicking niceties of an artificial, impersonal point system that he or she doesn't understand.

These problems are not inevitable. If they do occur, they can be dealt with. But they are an argument, at least, against specialists—or perhaps just against ineffective specialists.

EVALUATION COMMITTEES

As an alternative to using specialists, some companies appoint a job evaluation committee. Its members are fairly high-level managers drawn from various parts of the organization. Equipped with a working knowledge of jobs in their own areas and trained in the JE system, these managers both assist and offset one another in arriving at fair and rational evaluations. A committee should certainly be less susceptible to pressure and overruling than an individual.

Job evaluation by committee can be beneficial in other ways. The members get to know jobs throughout the company. They may discover either duplications or absences of accountabilities. Through job analysis they may see the way to more efficient or less costly ways of doing things—by means of reorganization, concentration of like functions, or elimination of unnecessary activities. And a greater knowledge of companywide job requirements may enable them to improve career planning for their own employees.

A committee reinforces confidence in the system. Employees know that evaluations are based on the group process, not on individual opinion. They know that companywide interests are represented. They know that someone familiar with their own jobs had a voice in decisions. A further benefit: in a small organization group participation develops a sense of mutual responsibility for the future of the company.

Some companies that use a committee also appoint a JE specialist to support the committee. The specialist can save committee time by obtaining job descriptions, keeping the records, and even preparing suggested evaluations for committee approval. The specialist can also provide a tentative "quickie" evaluation when necessary as a stopgap until the committee sits.

Even at its most demanding, job evaluation is a relatively safe process. Ghastly mistakes are not likely to occur. Gross underevaluation of a job will not go unnoticed. The worst that can happen is overevaluation, due to either a careless or a consistently overruled evaluator. Committee evaluation helps to prevent this.

Because position evaluation is an adjunct of salary administration, careful records should be kept. These include:

1. Files of current and obsolete descriptions.
2. Listings of job titles and numbers in ranking order (by points, if points are used).
3. Rankings of jobs under each evaluation factor, as an aid in determining the factor value of new jobs.
4. Dates and reasons supporting each evaluation. ("Level 4 of Knowledge was assigned to this position because . . . .")

Since the names of incumbents should have no bearing on position evaluation, these need not be part of the file.

JOB GRADES

Once the points for a job (or its ranking) have been determined, the result may be converted into a salary by means of a formula or wage curve. Some companies translate points directly into salaries. Thus a job with 210 points might carry a salary of $3,010 a month. One with 211 points might carry a salary minutely higher.

Other companies group jobs into grades, as illustrated below:

Points	Job Grade
0–49	1
50–99	2
100–149	3
150–199	4
200–249	5
250–299	6

For each grade, a salary or salary range exists. All positions falling in a given grade also fall into that salary bracket. (And of course, although the grades are fixed, the corresponding salaries may be revised from time to time to keep pace with the economy.)

Disclosure of Grades

Ordinarily employees are told what their job grade is. Frequently they are also informed of their salary range, which amounts to almost, but not quite, the same thing. Not quite the same because if you know that you are in grade 3, you have a very clear idea that there is a definite grade 4 above you. But you don't have a clear idea of what salary possibilities lie ahead.

Generally, it is not a good idea to disclose point assignments to employees. This is especially true under a job grade system. For example, suppose that your job carries 98 points, falling in job grade 2 in the table shown above. What is the first thing you think of? How to get two more points added to your job so that it will fall in job grade 3. Thinking about this does nothing for the company's benefit.

Once employees know their job points, it is a natural step for them to want to know how the points were arrived at. Soon the company is dotted with amateur job evaluators. The appointed evaluators then find that considerable time is taken up reviewing and explaining evaluations—in fact, defending and arguing them. Out of this tug-of-war inevitably come revisions, always upward.

Those revisions can be expensive. If all jobs were revised upward by the same amount, no harm would be done; the wage curve could be adjusted inversely. More likely, however, the most vocal and aggressive individuals will present convincing, or at least brain-wearying, arguments and win their cases. Others will not. The concentration of jobs will move toward the higher grades. All this costs the company money and channels time and energy away from the true objectives of the organization.

When salaried employees are unionized, their representatives will probably want access to the evaluation process, including, of course, the point assignments for jobs. Since widespread diffusion of this information will create the same problems for the union as it does for the company, a policy of confidentiality should be advocated and adhered to. (With changing union officials, however, this may not be easy to enforce.)

Some people may argue that all employees should be familiarized with the JE system and informed of the points of their own and other positions as evidence of fairness and good faith. Is it not wrong to withhold from employees the information that bears on so important a matter as pay? To this it may be answered that in knowing their salary range they do know the thing of most importance. As for the points or their derivation, it is not possible for the untutored employee to make intelligent judgments on them. Job evaluation is a skill that requires not only training in the system but also experience in its use on many jobs. Attempting to apply it without such training, and to a single job—the employee's own—cannot yield reliable results. The impartial evaluator looks at any job in the context of many. The employee is apt to evaluate his job with full appreciation of its own requirements and much less for those of other jobs. The employee is not fully informed on them and doesn't care about them. He is apt to try to milk the system for all he can get.

For these reasons a discussion of JE details is best avoided. At times, an employee or her supervisor may claim that the evaluation, as reflected in salary range, is too low. If investigation shows that the evaluation is in fact fair, a candid answer should be given. It may be that the real problem is one of placement: the salary is not too low for the job's demands; it is too low for the employee's abilities. A promotion to a more suitable position should be sought.

At other times a reverse allegation occurs. A supervisor objects to a salary range—and hence to the evaluation—as being too high. ("No way should the office clown be that high on the scale!") Once again, if the evaluation is found to be correct, it should be pointed out that it applies to the job, not the person. If the incumbent is performing the duties listed on the description, well and good. If not, who is? Is the description incorrect? Or if the duties are not being performed properly, why is the incumbent in that job?

SUMMARY

If your company is very small, a straight ranking system may well suffice. If your firm has as many as, say, 30 different salaried positions, you may wish to consider more analytical ranking systems, broken down into job factors. You probably won't want to invent your own. Some factor-point systems are available from trade associations. And there are proprietary systems available from consultants, some of which are supported with salary survey services.

4: SALARY STRUCTURE

JOB EVALUATION REFLECTS the internal relationships among jobs. These relationships must then be paralleled in a salary structure. The higher the evaluation of a position, the higher the salary.

RANGES

Salary structure has, in a way, two dimensions. The first dimension—which may be thought of as vertical—is the *range* of salaries for a given job. Thus the basic salary for a job (the term "basic" will be discussed later) is that rate of pay exactly corresponding to the job's evaluated ranking or points. The "range" is a spread of available salaries above and below this value. Somewhere in this range, the salaries of individual incumbents are assigned. This assignment depends on individual qualifications.

The range for a given point value—say, 390 points—might be as follows:

Maximum	$2,400 per month
Basic	$2,000 per month
Minimum	$1,600 per month

Figure I. Salary range spread.

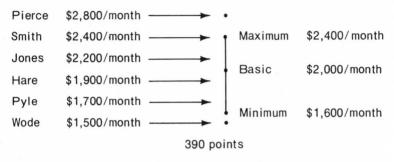

390 points

In this range there is a spread of 20 percent above and 20 percent below the basic value. The total spread is 40 percent around the midpoint, or 50 percent above the minimum.

Individual incumbents in a position may receive salaries at various points within the range. Consider a position evaluating at 390 points and having six incumbents, as illustrated in Figure 1. Smith, Jones, Hare, and Pyle all get something between the minimum ($1,600) and the maximum ($2,400). They are being treated according to policy.

Occasionally, however, exceptions are permitted to occur. Wode, in the illustration, is paid only $1,500 per month. Wode is outside the range—"below minimum." Perhaps Wode has been promoted from a much lower job and is being taken up to this job's salary in steps. Perhaps Wode is on probation and will be brought into the range after he demonstrates competence. Below-minimum salaries of this kind are a possible source of grievance. ("The work's getting done, isn't it?" says Wode.)

Pierce, on the other hand, is paid $2,800 per month—"above maximum." Assuming that Pierce does in fact hold the same position as the others, why is Pierce making more? There may be a number of reasons. Perhaps Pierce's former, higher-paying job was discontinued and Pierce was transferred downward to this one. Perhaps Pierce was demoted and the company, rather than cut her pay, decided to carry Pierce at the old salary until inflation moved the range up to encompass the $2,800. Again, Pierce may be so highly qualified that she has progressed to the maximum of the range some time ago. The company has continued to give Pierce salary increases in order to avoid losing her.

Salaries above the maximum are known as red-circle rates. They usually go to employees with long service or outstanding qualifications—employees whom the company does not wish to lose.

Smith, at $2,400 per month, is now receiving the maximum. Normally, unless the range changes or Smith is an exception like Pierce, Smith will not get further salary increases on this job. Smith seems to be ready for a promotion to a higher-paying job.

We have spoken of this range as though it applied to a single position. But it need not. *Any* job having 390 points would carry this salary range. If the positions of assets accountant, fibers chemist, and warehouse supervisor, all in the same company location, happened to evaluate at 390 points, each would fall in the salary range of $1,600 to $2,400 per month. Jobs evaluated at 395 points might fall in a higher salary range—say, $1,620 to $2,430. Those at 385 would have a lower range—say, $1,580 to $2,370.

Why a Range?

Why have a range of possible salaries for a given job? Why not have, instead, a specified salary for each job, and stick to it?

On some readily learned jobs, this may make sense. You hire someone as an inventory records clerk. Within a few weeks the new employee has learned to do the job as well as it can ever be done. If not, you get someone else. All your inventory records clerks are paced by the work. Whether they have been with you for a month or a decade, whether they are dense or brilliant, makes little difference on this job. Either they can do it or they can't. You pay them all the same salary. Once a year you give them all a raise, if necessary, to keep their pay in line with the going rates for such work. Well and good.

On more complex jobs there are more variables. Say you have three shift supervisors in your shop. One has only recently been promoted to the job. She still has a lot to learn, and when she has learned it she will feel she is worth more money to you. Another has been on the job ten years and does it acceptably. A third has been on the job only five years but is the best supervisor you have ever employed—no labor problems, high productivity, practically no spoilage losses, that sort of thing. Clearly it is good business to pay the star performer a relatively high salary in order to hold on to her, and to pay the tyro a relatively low salary with the opportunity to earn more. Yes, they are all on the same job, but the range of salaries for this job sensitizes the pay to their qualifications.

Going back now to the clerks, you might conceivably want to provide a salary range in this job for very general reasons. Perhaps it is a training ground for a higher position and salary progression will encourage people to stay around. Or you may feel that it is just good practice to pay older employees something more than novices. Custom enters into the matter also. Many employees who would take for granted a fixed rate for an hourly job would also take for granted a pay range if the same job were on salary.

GRADES

As mentioned in Chapter 3, some employers, rather than have a salary range peculiar to each evaluation, group jobs

Figure 2. Salary grade spread.

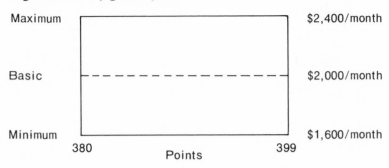

into grades, classes, brackets, or levels. Grades, to select one term, constitute the horizontal dimension of the salary structure. Thus, to continue our example, the salary range of $1,600 to $2,400 might apply to all jobs between 380 and 400 points, as shown in Figure 2.

Advantages of Grades

Grouping jobs into grades has several advantages:

1. It facilitates periodic adjustment of the salary ranges. For example, if the ranges are to be adjusted upward by 6 percent to recognize changes in market conditions, a set of ten grades requires a limited number of calculations. If, on the other hand, each job or point evaluation carries its own separate range, much more arithmetic must be performed to recalculate each range 6 percent higher. Today this advantage, which may have been one of the original reasons for using grades, has been nullified by the computer, which can adjust any number of ranges through a simple algorithm.

2. It recognizes that evaluation is an approximation at best. A job with 385 points is hard to distinguish from one with 386 or 387 points. Grouping the jobs with close evaluations provides as much precision as is necessary.

3. It provides a convenient, readily understood means of communicating the relative status of positions without getting into discussions of points. A job "is in grade 5" or it "is in grade 6."

4. It provides an easy way to identify promotions. If someone moves from a grade 5 to a grade 6 job, that is a promotion.

Problems with Grades

Job grades also present difficulties:

1. If they have the advantage of clustering jobs with nearby evaluations, they also have the disadvantage of separating "close" jobs that fall across the breakpoint of the ranges. Thus, in our example, a job with 379 points ends up a whole grade less than one with 380 points. If these two jobs are similar, or if the holder of the 379-point job discovers that it is "high in its grade," you will face efforts to have it moved up a notch.

2. Because the number of grades is limited, there is a tendency for them to become generally known. In fact, some companies, especially those with unions, publish them. This, too, leads to job comparisons and requests for upgrading. ("If that job is grade 6, mine should be grade 6 too.") Often these requests are based on incomplete information about the nature of other jobs.

3. The stark clarity of a limited number of grades encourages supervisors to do their own evaluating: "We are creating a new job in my department, and it should be in grade 9." Maybe it should and maybe it shouldn't. Perhaps the supervisor has plans to transfer someone into this job from a grade 8 position and hopes to make the move a promotion. In any case, grades encourage impressionistic rather than rational evaluation.

To minimize haggling for "upgrades" and similar problems, you can do away with grades completely. Employees, rather than being told that their job is in such-and-such a grade, can be informed of their salary range, which is what counts anyway.

As for promotion, you can define it as any move that results in a basic salary X percent higher than the basic salary of the incumbent's previous position.

Number of Grades

Some companies have as few as 10 grades, others as many as 30. Since grading and salary ranges can, and should, be applied to every position from the chief officer on down, it is clear that the number of grades will depend on the number of hierarchical levels in the company. Thus a small manufacturing company whose owner is chairman, president, and general manager may have only 10 grades. Some of these grades may in fact be blank, having no jobs at all at the present level of operations. A multinational firm with companies inside companies, like a nest of boxes, would have many grades.

And yet, even two essentially similar companies may have a different number of grades. A larger number of grades offers the following advantages:

1. It is more satisfactory to employees if movement between jobs of slightly different demand is reflected in salary differentials. More grades means more steps.

2. It is motivating to array certain types of jobs in a series based on increasing service, difficulty, or proficiency—for example, chemist D, chemist C, chemist B, chemist A, the last being highest. This multiplies the number of grades.

3. Numerous grades with small differentials obviate the need for large promotional increases.

4. Career advancement can be extended through a greater number of steps.

The ultimate extreme of this practice, of course, is to have a grade, if we may look at it that way, for every evaluation—to compute basic salary directly from evaluated points of whatever value.

In favor of fewer grades are the following:

1. A small number of grades is easier to administer from a recordkeeping viewpoint.

2. The more that jobs are clustered, the less likely that problems will arise from either alleged evaluation error or slight changes in duties.

3. Movement from a job in one grade to one in the next-higher grade is a significant advancement, clearly recognizable, and appropriately accompanied by a promotional increase.

4. When the jumps from grade to grade are large, there will be fewer instances of overlap, with people in widely different grades getting the same actual salaries. Hence there should be fewer complaints about inequities. ("I'm in grade 11 and I happen to know that my salary isn't any higher than my brother-in-law's, a grade 9 job. Do you call that fair?")

SALARY CURVES

When the basic salaries are plotted against evaluated points on a graph, you have a salary curve (so called even though it is a straight line). Figure 3 is an example. If you know the points of a job, you can read the basic salary from the curve. In this illustration, if no position in the evaluation plan has fewer than 100 points, the effective range of the curve lies between points A and B.

But a single curve like that in Figure 3 may not meet your needs. Perhaps jobs filled from the local market fall in a lower salary grouping than those that must be recruited from the national market—say, those of professional people. Also, if your company operates at several locations, you may have to pay relatively higher salaries in cities like New York and San Francisco than in small towns in the Southwest. As a result, there may be several salary curves (see Figure 4).

For convenience in calculating salaries, each curve may be expressed as a formula. For example, for professional jobs in low-cost-of-living cities, the formula may be:

$$\text{Basic salary} = \$50 + (\$4.5 \times \text{points})$$

(A caution: you will, of course, be sure that you do not set up separate curves for "male jobs" and "female jobs.")

When salary *grades* are used, these can be shown on the curve as steps (see Figure 5). Again, though the line consists of a flight of steps, it is called a salary curve. Thus all jobs in grade 3 have a basic salary of $1,500. If there are separate curves for various job groups, each would have its own "staircase."

The illustrations thus far have shown only basic, or midpoint, salaries. But ranges too can be displayed, as shown in Figure 6. The distance between the bottom and top of each block represents the salary range for the grade in question, which is 20 percent above and 20 percent below the midpoint, or basic, salary.

Still another variation is possible. The number of evaluation points included within a grade may increase with ascending job rank. Thus grade 1 might run from 87 to 112 points, while grade 10 might encompass 872 to 1,127 points. Why? Because the lower-ranking jobs are more clearly defined, easily differentiated, and limited in content than the higher general management jobs. This situation is depicted in Figure 7. Each grade has a 20 percent salary spread around the midpoint. In addition, the width of the grade blocks (in points) increases by a constant percentage, so that the higher

Figure 3. Straight-line salary curve.

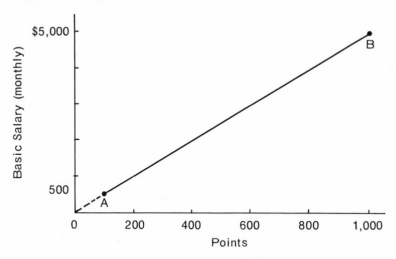

Figure 4. Multiple salary curves.

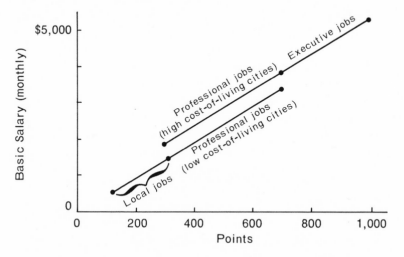

Figure 5. Stepped salary curve.

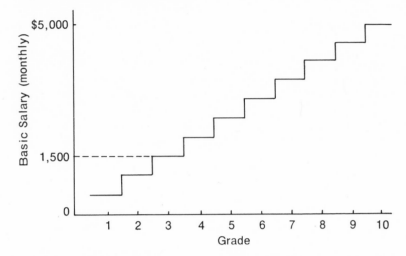

grades encompass more points. The average dollar value per point is uniform in all grades.

While this profusion of salary curves may seem confusing, it has been presented for a reason. It reflects the variety found in actual practice. There is no uniformity of salary curves among companies. Nor is there any right or wrong curve. Too many variables are involved. The general slope of the salary curve for your company will probably relate to that of other companies. But in all other respects you may find differences reflecting company policy, practice, and preference.

SALARY RANGE OVERLAP

Salary ranges customarily overlap. Thus the ranges for two adjacent grades would look, not like situation A in Figure 8 but like situation B, where the midpoint of grade 4 is somewhat above that of grade 3. They may even look like situation

Figure 6. Stepped salary curve with ranges.

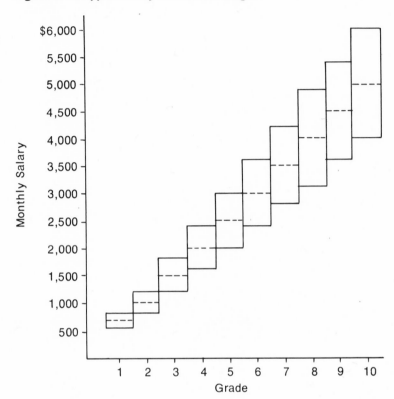

C, where the midpoint of grade 4 is higher than the maximum of grade 3.

Situation B prevails when there are many grades. An upward transfer from one grade to the next represents only a small change.

Situation C is common when there are fewer grades. Consider a person at the midpoint of the lower grade: $800 a month. Presumably, if transferred to the next-higher job, the employee would initially be less proficient on the new as-

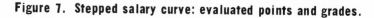

Figure 7. Stepped salary curve: evaluated points and grades.

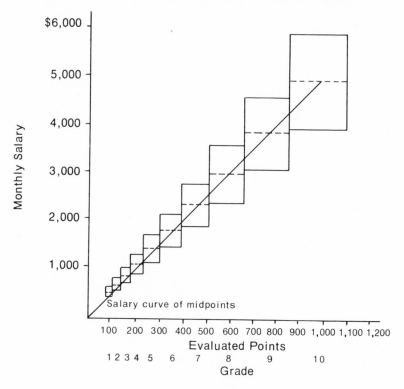

signment than on the old one, and hence not qualified for the new basic salary. A 5 percent promotional increase would still leave room for subsequent upward movement in the range of the new job. We will examine this question of position in range in a later chapter.

One effect of overlap is that an employee in the upper range of, say, grade 3 may be making a higher salary than an employee in the lower range of grade 4. Depending on the qualifications of the two employees, this may be perfectly

Figure 8. Salary range overlap.

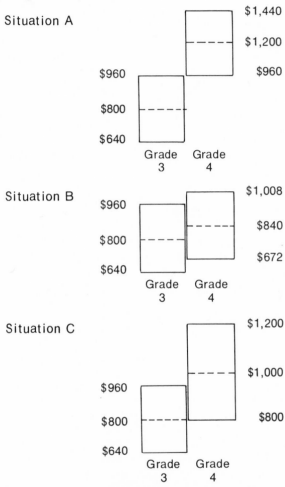

reasonable. The high grade 3 employee may be a person of long service and exceptional competence, while the low grade 4 employee may be relatively new and inexperienced on the job.

Compression

Compression exists when the earnings of lower-evaluated jobs are very close to those of higher-evaluated ones to which they have a reporting or promotional relationship. Suppose, for example, that a supervisor's salary is $1,200 a month, and the monthly earnings, including overtime and bonus, of certain hourly employees reporting to that supervisor are $1,190 a month. The compensation of the supervisor and the supervised are too close together.

One effect of such compression is a strong sense of injustice on the part of the supervisor: "Look what the union does for its members! What does the company do for me?" Maybe, he thinks, he needs a union too.

A second effect is a reluctance on the part of hourly employees to accept promotion to supervisory positions. Nothing, they think, is to be gained except loss of security. It is a generally accepted convention that supervisors receive 15 to 20 percent more than the highest-paid hourly employee under them.

Another form of compression exists when salary increases for older employees have not kept pace with increases in hiring rates. It may turn out that a marketing assistant, for example, is being hired right out of school for almost as much money as a product manager who has three years of service. When that product manager learns of this, he or she begins to send out résumés.

CLARIFICATION OF TERMS
Basic Salary and Midpoint

The terms "midpoint" and "basic salary" are by no means unambiguous. Certainly the midpoint of the range is clearly defined. It is the salary determined from the salary curve as equivalent to the evaluated level of the job. But what does that signify?

To some it represents the salary that an experienced, qualified person of average competence should receive for doing that job. To others it may represent merely the level to which all the going salaries being paid within the company, in that range, should average. To still others it may represent the average of all salaries for that bracket in the area or in the nation at a specified time. (If the midpoints of the salary curve were determined from a survey, that is indeed what it is.) Or it may be some predetermined percentage of that average— say, 110 percent if the company is a "high pay" outfit, 90 percent if it is a "low pay" firm.

Minimum Salary and Maximum Salary

Both the minimum and maximum salaries are also open to interpretation. Some companies view them merely as arbitrary limits to the range. They are a percentage below and a percentage above, nothing more. Other companies interpret them in a more specific, definitive sense. Thus the minimum is defined as the salary to be given to an employee who is starting on the job without previous experience. And if midpoint, or basic, is the salary for an experienced person who demonstrates normal competence, then the maximum may be defined as the rate of pay for incumbents of clearly superior ability. Under another interpretation, the maximum may be associated, not with superior ability but with tenure in the company.

Effect on Employees

Failure to clarify the meaning of terms may affect how your employees react to the salary system. For example, use of the term "midpoint" suggests to the employee that this position is a way station on the journey to the maximum of the range. But suppose that this is not the case at all. Suppose the employer intends midpoint—more accurately "basic salary" in this case—to represent the proper pay for employees of sufficient competence to do the job satisfactorily. Then, by definition, only superior employees would progress beyond it. Most employees would not get into the upper half of the salary range. They would then feel deprived of an opportunity for further increases beyond the halfway point. "Midpoint" would be a misleading—in fact mischievous—locution. For most employees it would be endpoint.

Suppose, then, that to avoid misconceptions, the company uses the word "basic." And suppose that "basic" is described as the salary for employees of normal, expected competence. As noted before, employees who are indeed of average competence or who are doing essentially the same work as others receiving higher pay will have an argument in favor of being immediately brought up to the "basic" level. What do years of experience or service matter if the employees are getting the work done?

Considering that many jobs can be performed adequately with less than a year's experience—especially by people who have graduated into them from other, lower jobs—a good many employees would probably qualify for the "basic" or "standard" rate under this interpretation. After all, the business is not in the hands of employees who are less than competent.

But hustling everyone rapidly from minimum to basic poses two problems. First, it means higher costs to the company than would otherwise occur. Second, it means that most employees, having quickly risen to the basic salary, have little opportunity to move further (unless they get promoted to a higher position). The carrot has suddenly disappeared. Most salary administrators consider this cessation of motivational pay increases to be psychologically unsound.

A sounder approach is to base movement through the range on years of experience—or, better yet, on years of experience with demonstrated competency. (This is a subject in itself and will be discussed under "merit increases" in Chapter 5.) The point here is that the significance of the company's salary structure and salary terminology must be thoroughly understood.

In the rest of this book we will refer to midpoint, basic, or standard salaries, letting the meaning follow the context.

THE SMALL ESTABLISHMENT

Preoccupied with orders, cash flow, and deliveries, the proprietor of the small establishment may feel that adding a spiderweb of salary curves to the complexities of the business is adding just a little too much. Yet once-a-year attention to salary range architecture serves a useful purpose. By bringing system and order to salary management, it lessens preoccupation with personnel problems throughout the year.

Drawing the salary curve on graph paper helps to visualize the salary structure. Of course, a simpler alternative is to prepare a listing, as shown in Table 1. Such a tabulation gives

TABLE 1
Salary grades and ranges.

Grade		Salary Range		
No.	Points	Minimum	Midpoint	Maximum
1	200–249	$ 400	$ 500	$ 600
2	250–314	800	1,000	1,200
3	315–394	1,200	1,500	1,800
4	395–489	1,600	2,000	2,400
5	490–600	2,000	2,500	3,000

the proprietor a good sense of proportion in dealing with questions of hiring salaries, increases, and promotions in specific cases. It is the kind of thing that makes a business businesslike.

PROBLEMS AND RISKS

There are a number of problems or risks in the design of a salary structure.

Insufficient Range Spread. If the salary range for, say, chemical engineers is only 10 percent above and below the midpoint, there is not much room to accommodate differences in the ability or tenure of various individuals. Old-timers at the maximum will not be making much more than newcomers at the minimum.

Excessive Range Spread. If there is a 25 percent range spread above and below the average salary of, say, keypunch operators, the inevitable migration of employees into the high end of the range means that you will probably end up paying too much for this relatively standardized type of work. Also, since district pay levels for such work tend to cluster fairly closely, the "minimum" of the range, which should be the starting rate, is probably unrealistic—too far below average to attract anyone.

Too Few Salary Curves. Whether one or several salary curves should be used depends on the size of the company, the diversity of its jobs, and the geographical distribution of its operations. A single, continuous salary curve does not provide for disparities that occur in the real world. Thus the curves for executive, professional, and clerical jobs may be different in slope and point coverage.

Salary curves in high-cost-of-living areas may be necessarily higher than in other areas.

Use of Job Grades. As mentioned earlier, grouping jobs into grades based on clusters of evaluations has its pros and cons. In a general sense, it facilitates salary administration and makes salary actions more comprehensible to employees. But it also accentuates pay disparities between similar jobs that fall on opposite sides of the grade breaks.

Too Few Grades. An insufficient number of grades for the spectrum of positions creates two problems. First, it does not provide enough pay differential for jobs that are in fact different. Second, it suppresses promotional recognition. A person moving from one position to another of manifestly higher requirements may stay in the same grade, and hence in the same salary range. The psychological (as well as monetary) reward of "moving up" is lost.

Compression. Rising earnings of hourly employees dictate an increase in the salary range of their immediate supervisors. But this increase in turn ripples up to *their* supervisors. Adjustment of these ranges all the way up the pyramid—perhaps by means of a separate salary curve for supervisors—throws these salaries out of line with the salaries of related professionals, such as factory accountants and engineers.

5: SALARY RANGE

IN THIS CHAPTER we will examine the salary range more closely. What is it? Why is there a range? What determines where employees fall in the range? How do they progress upward?

BASIC ASSUMPTIONS

For the sake of our analysis, let us make certain assumptions. Suppose, in our consideration of salary range, that we stipulate a world in which:

- There is no inflation. Whatever the salary range for a given job is this year, it will remain so for all years to come.
- There is no change in company sales or profits. The money available for salaries will not increase as a result of more output per employee.
- There is absolute fairness and equity in fitting salaries to individuals. No one is paid "outside the rules." No one obtains an increase in pay because of threats to quit, favoritism, or even simple errors in the supervisor's judgment.
- A set of rules exists governing the timing and amount of salary increases. These rules are as follows:
  1. All employees newly placed on jobs who do not have

Figure 9. Salaries within range.

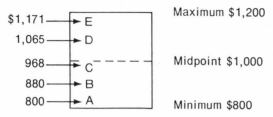

previous experience in such jobs shall receive the
minimum rate in a given bracket. This is the starting
rate.

2. Each employee shall, on the anniversary of starting
the job, receive a merit increase of 10 percent, provided acceptable performance is demonstrated.
(Since we have stipulated a noninflationary environment, this is a merit increase—not to be confused
with the so-called cost-of-living increase, which will
be discussed in a later chapter.)

3. No employee shall receive more than the maximum
of the range.

To illustrate, consider the salary range shown in Figure 9.
A, B, C, D, and E are employees receiving the salaries shown.
Employee A, at $800, receives the minimum of the range.
Presumably, A has been on the job for less than twelve
months. Employee B has been on the job in this range for at
least a year. B has been given a 10 percent merit increase
over the starting rate and now makes $880.

Employee C has apparently been on the job for two to
three years. C has had two increases since starting, and these
two 10 percents have brought C to $968. C is practically at
the midpoint. Employee D, at $1,065, has gone one step fur-
ther. Employee E has been on the job long enough, and with

sufficiently good performance, to rise to $1,171, almost at the maximum. No more 10 percent raises for E.

In this situation the employees' salaries are fairly evenly distributed throughout the range. The average salary is not far from the midpoint.

DISPERSION VERSUS COSTS

The degree to which an even salary dispersion is maintained has an effect on company costs. For example, suppose that as employees reach the maximum of the range they either retire or move to a job in a higher range. As they do, they are replaced by others at the starting rate. The dispersion will remain stable, and the average cost of employees in this bracket will remain unchanged.

On the other hand, suppose that few employees retire on reaching the top of the range—after all, from start to top takes only four years of annual increases. And suppose that they don't get promoted out, either because they lack qualifications or because openings are scarce. In a few years all employees will be clustered at the high end of the range. As a result, even in the absence of economic inflation, the payroll will go up.

Unless there is fairly normal turnover—people leaving jobs and others entering them—a rule of periodic increases escalates payroll costs.

Slowing down the rate of progression retards but does not eliminate the rate of growth. For example, the 10 percent per year that we have used is unrealistically high. Suppose it were reduced to 3 percent a year. Then it would take over thirteen years for an employee who never changed jobs to advance from the starting rate to the maximum. Nevertheless, as all employees move through the range in this fashion, with no turnover, the center of gravity will eventually shift, with the average salary well above the midpoint.

Management puzzled by a payroll rise may therefore wish to consider if low turnover is a contributing factor. It can be one cause of an uneven salary dispersion.

MERIT INCREASES

Increases of the type just described—those responsive to internal policies rather than to external economic events—are commonly called "merit increases." Although they are often taken for granted, the reasons for them are worth examining. Why give merit increases at all?

Before answering this question, let us consider the midpoint, or basic, salary again. The midpoint is determined from surveys of salaries paid by others. Just as a company must pay the going rates for the fuels, utilities, and raw materials that it uses, so must it expect to pay "going" rates for people. How these rates are arrived at is described in the next chapter. For the present purpose, let us add to our list of assumptions one more:

- For jobs like those in a given range, the midpoint of the range is equal to the average going rate of pay in the community (the population, local or nationwide, in which the company competes for employees).

Now among the employees in the large external survey group, there is a dispersion of salaries. Some traffic rate clerks, for example, make more than this average; some make less. Presumably, those who make more have longer experience, greater familiarity with the scope of their work, and higher skill. As a result, they have a greater value to the company, such that the employer would rather pay them a higher salary than replace them with lower-cost clerks.

At the other end of the scale are the lower-paid clerks. They are probably newer, younger, less skilled, more needful of supervision—in short, more expendable—for otherwise they would be able to bargain for more money either from their present employer or from another employer.

If we consider the average of all these external rates to be the midpoint, then our survey universe should show an even dispersion about the midpoint, with roughly as many people above as below. In our own company, then, assuming there is a similar difference among individual qualifications, we may expect a corresponding spread. Merit increases, by moving people through the range, create this spread.

Thus an employee who shows normal progress on a job must be given periodic increases in order to be retained by the company. Otherwise, with accumulating skill, the employee could earn more in another company. So our rate clerk, starting with no practice on the job, begins at the starting rate. At suitable intervals—perhaps six months at the start and a year thereafter—the clerk is given a merit increase.

Now we can return to our question: Why grant merit increases? (Not cost-of-living increases, let it be remembered, but merit increases.) The answer, of course, is to retain competent employees.

EMPLOYEE RETENTION

An employee, when newly placed on a job, is offered a starting salary. At this point the employee theoretically has the option of accepting the position at this salary or rejecting it. If the employee is inexperienced on this job, the starting rate is competitively fair. The employee is unlikely to get a better offer elsewhere. Assume, then, that the job is accepted at the starting rate. A year or so passes and the employee gains some familiarity with and skill at the job. With these qualifications, he or she could now apply to another company for a salary closer to the general average. In order to avoid starting another beginner, the employer must therefore raise the present employee's salary.

This, then, is the general rationale for merit increases. They are necessary in order to retain employees who are acquiring, within the company, the ability to command a higher salary for their abilities.

This principle, though true in a broad sense, may not apply in individual cases. For example, certain employees may be unlikely to leave the company even if they do not get a merit increase. They are immobilized, so to speak, for any one of several reasons:

- Family problems that necessitate staying in the locality.
- Emotional inability to face the risk of a change in employment.
- Loyalty to the organization to which they belong.
- Personal characteristics that make it difficult for them to "sell" themselves to another employer (stuttering, for a trivial example).
- Skills that are in either such small demand or such great supply that there is no competitive market for them.
- Expectations of future promotion or rise in the company.

If it is true that some employees can be retained even without merit increases, it is equally true that others cannot be held even with them. Your company may religiously give increases when earned, and still lose employees. These employees may drift away because your company:

- Does not offer the career opportunities they expect.
- Has an atmosphere or management style distasteful to them.

- Has an inconvenient geographical location or unpleasant working facilities.
- Does not provide a sense of employment security.

Many other reasons could be cited. Nevertheless, whether merit increases seem superfluous in some cases or inadequate in others, they are an essential feature of a program involving salary ranges.

DEGREE OF SPREAD

The spread of a range—that is, the difference between the maximum and minimum salary—varies with the nature of the jobs covered by the range.

Some jobs are fairly elementary. For example, the duties of an accounting keypunch operator can be learned in a short time. Years and years of experience at this job do not add much to proficiency. Accordingly, the midpoint is not far above the starting rate. Keypunch operator is in a job grade at the lower end of the salary curve, where salaries tend to group more closely around an average.

Other jobs require relatively greater experience for midpoint or maximum salary qualifications. For example, a top-notch plant electrical engineer is far more knowledgeable than a beginner. He or she knows far more equipment—its design, its suppliers, its problems, its layout, and its use in the factory. To reach this degree of proficiency may take substantial time. More merit increases may lie between starting and maximum for such work. The growth, the spread of the range, is greater. A survey of other employers will show a wide dispersion of salaries in these upper brackets.

If lower-level jobs have a spread of 20 to 25 percent, professional and managerial jobs may have a spread of 40 to 50 percent. That is to say, an employee with top qualifications and experience would make around 50 percent more than one who is a beginner on the job.

TIMING AND AMOUNT OF INCREASE

We have spoken of merit increases as if they were a fixed percentage. Actually they vary, both with different jobs and with different employees. The timing of merit increases also varies. The period between increases may be shrunk or expanded to suit individual conditions.

Job Rank or Grade. Merit increases vary with the position of the job in the overall ranking. As mentioned earlier, jobs at the lower end of the curve have a shallower salary range, and hence a shorter trip between min and max. Rather than give two or three increases across this traverse, some companies prefer to give several smaller increases, over a longer period of time. Jobs at the upper end of the curve may, by contrast, receive a larger percentage increase per time period. There is more ground to be covered. Thus the keypunch operator may get a merit increase of 2 percent, while the plant electrical engineer gets 4 percent. The latter position has a min that is farther from midpoint to begin with.

Performance. Merit increases also vary with individual performance. Employees whose performance exceeds expectations receive a higher merit increase percentage than do average employees. Consider the grade occupied by the position of plant electrical engineer, for which we postulated a normal merit increase of 4 percent. Say this 4 percent is applicable to all employees whose performance meets normal expectations. Then an individual who exceeds normal job requirements for people at the given position in the range might receive a 5 percent increase. One who far exceeds the requirements might receive 6 percent.

The timing of increases, too, may vary with performance. Those employees who do better than the average may be given not only a higher merit increase but a quicker one. In contrast, employees who do not come up to expectations may be given a subnormal increase, and at longer intervals. Or no increase.

Position in Range. Employees in the lower part of the salary range may be "raised" more frequently than those in the upper part. Why? Because it is during the early years on the job that employees move most rapidly from a learning phase to a competence phase. Once they have demonstrated full competence and have reached the midpoint, further progress (according to one view) consists of a gradual broadening of experience. It occurs more slowly. On a more practical basis, once they are past the midpoint, there are fewer competitors' jobs to which they may be lured. They are now entering the area of above-average earnings for what they do. For these reasons, some employers provide for a longer interval between increases as employees move up in the range.

EFFECT OF MERIT INCREASE

A merit increase, once given, has an effect on salary, and hence costs, persisting long after the year in which it is granted. Consider two employees, A and B, both receiving $1,000 a month. A's performance is judged satsifactory. An increase of 4 percent is given, bringing A's salary to $1,040. B's performance is judged superior. An increase of 6 percent is given, bringing B's salary to $1,060. In the next few years, each employee's performance is found to be satisfactory and each receives a 4 percent increase each year.

Figure 10 shows the results after six years. The height of the line indicates ongoing salary. As the figure indicates, a high merit rating in a single year boosts the employee's earn-

Figure 10. Effect of merit increase.

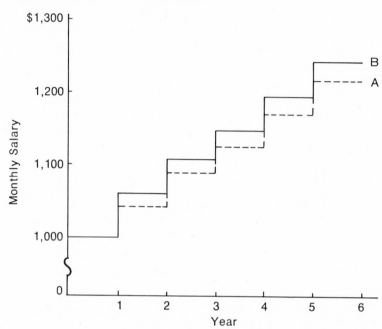

ings for all subsequent years. This happens even though performance in those years is no more than average.

Some thought should therefore be given to the meaning and purpose of merit increases. The purpose should be to move the employee into a range position justified by overall, ongoing performance. If this guideline is observed, merit increase would not be given as a "reward" for spurts of atypical activity.

Suppose that a very average employee (average in terms of overall ability) pitches in with exceptional vigor to help get a new billing system installed. Better that this extra effort be compensated with a special one-time payment than that the employee be moved, for all time to come, into a range position inconsistent with that of others. One can imagine a conversation in the future: "Why does Smith make more money than the rest of us? He doesn't seem outstanding to me." "Well, he helped install a new billing system five years ago." "Yes, and we don't even use it anymore."

As Sir Francis Bacon said in an essay ("On Expense") in 1607: "A man ought warily to begin charges which once begun must contynue. But in matters that retourne not, hee may be more magnificent."

A program of merit increases is sometimes said to be justified for "motivation." Presumably, employees will tote more bales in the hope of getting a raise as a reward. Maybe so. But if this is the only means the supervisor has of getting work done well, the company is in difficulty. In the real world, employees come to expect merit increases as long as their performance is adequate. Whether employees do adequate work is as much a matter of selection, training, and management as it is of motivation. The most a merit program can realistically hope to achieve is motivation to stay on as an employee.

PROBLEMS AND RISKS

For the orderly administration and control of salaries it is necessary to establish only two general laws:

- There shall be a set of company rules setting forth exactly how individual salaries are to be determined and how increases are to be granted.
- All salaries and changes therein shall conform to these rules.

Unfortunately a third and more general law sets the first two at naught. It is:

• People will make ad hoc exceptions to all general laws.

This third rule, which incidentally animated the behavior of Copernicus and Al Capone, often creates problems in the sphere of salary administration. When "exceptions" are made, the symmetry of salaries within a range, the regularity of increases, and the control of overall salary levels become warped a little at a time—always for the best of reasons, but in a direction that ultimately distorts the order of the original plan. Several problems are discussed below.

Out-of-Line Hires. Your company needs one more intermediate programmer. From another firm you recruit one who is already making a salary close to the average of your own programmers of similar ability. As part of the recruiting effort you offer a salary better than the candidate could get with his or her present employer. Now this programmer comes aboard high in the salary range for intermediate programmers. When the others find out, they complain. They are just as skilled as the newcomer. In the meantime, you begin to wonder: How many increases can the new person receive in the future before bumping into the ceiling?

Or suppose the candidate is a real hotshot who will be of inestimable value to your company, and only your maximum salary will close the deal. Will future raises be withheld because the ceiling of the range has already been reached? Never, even though breaking the ceiling is against your policy and your rules.

In an effort to avoid solving an immediate vacancy problem by creating a long-range salary problem, some companies attract new, high-level employees by offering a sizable hiring bonus instead of a higher salary. "It's as good as two years' worth of raises. You get it all at once, and you'll still get normal merit increases." Of course, if the new hire leaves after a year, the bonus is money lost.

Red-Circle Salaries. For one reason or another, there are always a few employees who are getting salaries above the maximum for their range—red-circle rates. They get there in various ways:

- Downward transfer from a higher position.
- Carryover from the past before the present evaluations, salary curves, and ranges were established.
- Recognition of superstar status.
- Raises given to counteract a threat to quit for better pay elsewhere. (This is always a bad practice, except for really indispensable employees. And who is indispensable?)

The obvious solution to the red-circle problem is to promote employees to a position with a range that their salary will fit. Unless this can be done, a second problem arises: What about further merit increases—especially if employees are doing good work? Many firms withhold such increases until inflation raises the range maximum above the red-circle level. Others give red-circle employees inflation-reflecting increases. This does not change their status, but it at least keeps them moderately happy.

Some red-circle employees—a brilliant researcher, for example, or an all-around manager who can fill in on many jobs in an emergency—are on what amount to individual rates, determined more by personal ability than by simple job evaluation. For them full merit increases, even above the so-called maximum, may be justified.

Below-Minimum Salaries. Though "below minimum" may sound like a contradiction, there are times when certain incumbents do receive less than the nominal minimum. This is not a desirable condition. If employees are not in fact performing the duties called for in the job description, then a new description and evaluation should be prepared for whatever they are doing. For example, if the employee is a trainee on a job, it is preferable to establish a separate trainee position than to carry the person as an underpaid incumbent of the full job. Unless the distinction is kept clear on the records, the company could face charges of discrimination—unequal pay for what is in the books as the same work.

At times a person is promoted from a low-paying job to a much higher one. In our earlier example the purchasing agent retires and it turns out that his secretary, who has worked for him for years, can step into the boss's shoes with ease. But promotion would mean bringing her (we will assume that the secretary is a woman) up to at least the minimum pay for the position, a raise of over 100 percent. To some salary administrators there is something almost morally wrong in granting an increase of this magnitude. "Better to bring the secretary up with generous raises of 25 percent at a time, spread over a decent period." Obviously, however, this course lays the employer open to a charge of sex discrimination. And even if the secretary were a man, such a policy would still discriminate (though not legally) against the company's own loyal employees, since an outsider hired as purchasing agent would probably come in at least at the minimum rate.

Concentration. In companies, or even in departments, that have low turnover, employees tend to remain in their positions for many years. This situation may arise from various causes:

- The employees are still far from retirement age, though they have accumulated years of service.

- The employees perform a type of work for which there is little competitive demand, so they can't get jobs elsewhere.
- The employees are on what amounts to dead-end work, with few opportunities for promotion.
- The best employees have indeed resigned or been promoted in the past, so that through natural selection in reverse, only the mediocre are left.

One result of these events is that the employees are all concentrated in the top of the salary range, bobbing against the ceiling. Being effectively cut off from the merit increases they were accustomed to in the past, they become unhappy. Keeping them happy by giving them further merit increases will take them above the maximum; hence they will be highly paid compared with external averages for the same type of work. Who should bear this added cost: the customers, through higher prices, or the stockholders, through reduced profits? Poor people movement leads to salary problems.

Range Overlap. Salary ranges with too much overlap create problems when promotions occur. Consider an employee being promoted from grade 8 to grade 9 in a company where the maximum of the lower grade is equal to the midpoint of the higher grade (see Figure 11). It is entirely natural for an employee who is near the top of his or her grade to move to a higher job when a vacancy occurs. But in this structure the overlap of the grades is so great that the employee ends up fairly high in the range of the new job.

This situation, which is exacerbated by a promotional increase, causes two difficulties. First, there is little room for future "growth" of the employee's salary in the new job. Second, the employee is quite possibly receiving a higher salary than that of other employees who entered grade 9 by a differ-

Figure II. Salary range overlap: midpoint and maximum.

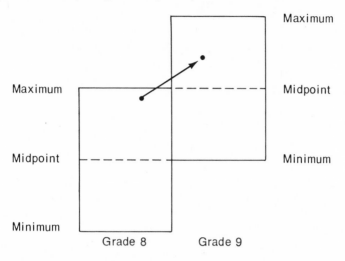

ent route. Less overlap of grades helps to prevent these problems.

THE SMALL ESTABLISHMENT

It may be thought that the smaller establishment can avoid
the problems described above by not setting up job salary
ranges in the first place. But in fact salary ranges are a form
of control. If you do not plan salaries, you will be at a competitive disadvantage with employers who do. You may lose
employees who naturally want the well-managed, reliable
salary opportunities that progressive, successful firms provide. By the same token, with a rangeless, unplanned salary
program you may end up with higher costs—having, say, the
world's highest-paid bookkeeping clerk. Being small does not
absolve you from following good business practice. But neither does good business practice absolve you from all problems.

6: SALARY SURVEYS

You want to know how your salaries stack up against those paid by other employers. Are they in line with your policy? Are you paying enough to hold on to good employees? What should you offer as a hiring rate to a new file clerk? Or to a young business administration graduate? If your salary expense has moved up in the last year, has the climb been parallel to that of other employers in your area or type of business? Can you believe what you read in the newspapers about increases—and what you hear through the employee grapevine? What is going on in that world outside the microcosm of your company?

TYPES OF SURVEYS

Questions like these are answered through salary surveys, which help employers keep in touch with their environment. Surveys may be company-initiated or they may be routinely executed by third parties such as trade associations and consulting firms. There are various types of surveys.

One type is a request directed (usually annually) to a number of employers asking them to report actual salaries for a list of identified jobs.

A second type, more limited, occurs when an employer needs data on the going salary rates for a specific type of job.

Say your employment department gets looks of disbelief when it makes an offer to applicants for the position of air pollution engineer. The proposed salary has been drawn from the range associated with your salary curve. But perhaps demand for this profession has created a temporary situation that the curve cannot accommodate. You may wish to survey salaries being paid by other companies for this type of work in order to find out if pollution control engineers are commanding a premium salary.

A third type of survey seeks information on general practice. For example, suppose that you don't want to go to the trouble of checking the competitive current salaries for a whole group of jobs. You feel that the internal relationship among your salaries is holding up well, and your only question is: "Are we in general, as a whole, keeping up with trends?" You are not alone. Many other employers have used surveys to obtain this type of information. Here is a sampling of questions from one survey:

1. How frequently do you increase salary ranges?
2. What was the average percentage range increase in each of the last five years?
3. What is the percentage spread between min and max of your lowest- and highest-level positions?
4. Do you give general increases? If so, how many and what percentage did you give in each of the last five years?
5. Do you plan to give another general increase? If so, when?
6. In the last twelve months what percentage did you average for general (range) increases, for merit increases, and for promotional increases?

General surveys are usually conducted annually. During inflation they are likely to result in an upward adjustment of the salary curve, thus raising the midpoint of the range for any given job. From this upward adjustment comes the necessity for giving employees "range adjustment" increases. These increases are intended to keep your company's salaries competitive with those of others. They are not merit increases. They are in addition to merit. As we shall see, they leave the employee's position in the range the same as before.

In this chapter we will examine the nature and use of surveys. We will discuss their application by employers who have a substantial number of salaried positions; we will also examine a shortcut method for employers who have only a few.

PURPOSE OF SURVEYS

A principal purpose of surveying outside salaries is to arrive at the height and slope of a salary curve that will keep you in line with your policy of paying the same as (or more or less than) your competitors in the labor market. Surveying helps you determine the dollar value of your salary range midpoints. Related purposes of surveys include:

- Checking to see what your hiring rates should be.
- Checking specific jobs that you have reason to think may have out-of-line salaries.
- Finding out what other companies have been averaging in merit increases, promotional increases, and general (or range adjustment) increases.
- Learning what the current practice is on the pay differential between supervisors and subordinates.
- Discovering trends in exempt overtime pay, area differentials, range spreads, and other salary-related matters.

AREA COVERED

The area covered by the survey is that in which your establishment must compete for employees. For positions in the lower earnings brackets—typically nonexempt positions—the survey may cover only the immediate community area. This is the sector from which you hire for these jobs.

For positions in higher brackets—typically executive, managerial, and professional jobs—the survey may be national in scope. Employees in such positions are mobile. When they are recruited by a company in another state, the new employer covers their relocation expenses. They can afford to move for a higher salary. Whether to attract them or retain them, you must know how your salaries compare on a national basis.

In between is a group of employees—typically supervisors and sometimes technicians—for which both local and national data are useful. If your supervisors, for example, have been promoted from the ranks, and their assets consist primarily of knowledge of company methods and people, they are apt to be locality-bound. Local surveys will tell you what the going rate is for them. If, on the other hand, your supervisor's chief assets are technical knowledge—or if you are in an expanding industry with a demand for specialized supervisors—then they are likely to be in the national market, so to speak. Broad survey data are essential.

Area differentials are an important aspect of salary competition. If you operate in New York City, you may expect to pay more for a given job than if you operate in Charleston. Local cost-of-living data (from the Bureau of Labor Statistics) are one way of determining area differentials, but area surveys of salaries paid are safer.

SOURCES OF INFORMATION

Salary survey data are obtained from a variety of sources. You don't have to initiate your own survey. The last thing anyone wants to see in the mail basket is another questionnaire. Better, hook in with an existing group that is already collecting the kind of information you need.

Local Interchange. Often a group of employers in a locality arranges for exchange of data on salaries, usually at the non-exempt and supervisory levels.

Trade Associations. Many industry trade associations have a service for collecting and disseminating comparable salary information to members. The American Bankers Association and the American Association of Museums provide such a service.

Professional Societies. Some professional societies—for example, the American Institute of Industrial Engineers—keep track of salaries paid for representative positions occupied by members and provide annual compilations.

Salary Services. A number of services exist to supply comparative salary information. Some of these cover the full gamut of positions; others cover those in a particular field. Foremost among them is the American Management Associations. In addition, there are consultants, universities, and independent associations that cover specific industries. Among the consultants, those that counsel on job evaluation methods and benefits programs frequently maintain an associated survey system.

One service, the College Placement Council (P.O. Box 2263, Bethlehem, PA 18001), issues periodic summaries of salary offers made to graduates in a number of curricula and includes bachelor's, master's, and doctoral degrees. The analysis is broken down by types of employers making the offer. Thus, if you are in the building industry, you can learn the average and range of offers being made to civil engineers.

Government. The Bureau of Labor Statistics of the Department of Labor issues periodic survey data on salaries for selected positions. (An example is presented later in the chapter.)

Commercial Publications. Some trade periodicals—*Infosystems,* for example—publish salary data for positions in their field. These surveys are often quite detailed. (An example is shown later in this chapter.)

Miscellaneous Sources. In addition to sources on the full range of positions, many sources can be tapped for salary data on specific positions. These include:

- Proxy statements—these show actual salaries of top executives.
- Executive search firms—behind these lie research agencies that accumulate organization charts and salaries of specific employees (not always accurate) for many companies.
- School placement offices—these are helpful on starting salaries, but they must be assessed judiciously.
- Help-wanted ads.
- Employment agencies.

The last two sources tend to run to the high side of salaries. After all, they are out fishing. Employees occasionally cite ad and agency figures as evidence that they are being underpaid.

INPUT DATA

The value of survey data is no better than the information fed into its collection system. In a good survey, each participant is given (1) a list of job titles being surveyed and (2) a job description (supplied by the organizing agency or by other participants) for each title. The description should be included to make sure that the salary reported by the respondent applies to the duties covered. Otherwise, the range of salaries for a title might be misleading.

For example, the scope of salaries paid to the position of programmer is extensive. It ranges from programmers updating simple compilations in Basic to those initiating new programs in dedicated languages on special-purpose scientific computers. How do you know where your own programmer should fall? Only a job description can ensure comparability of salaries.

A good survey also requests the actual salaries being paid on a given date for each position as well as the evaluated points for that position (if the participants share a common evaluation system). The survey should request the number of employees receiving each salary as well as additional data on bonuses, fringes, and hours of work. With some positions, typically those for salespeople and upper-level executives, the contribution of salary to total compensation varies greatly from company to company. Often a low salary goes with a high bonus. You should know whether the survey data used for determining your salary curve represent total cash compensation.

Method of Obtaining Data

On informal or spot surveys, you can get data through a phone call, a letter, or a visit. In most localities, and even nationally, there is a friendly network of people handling salaries. They find it mutually advantageous to exchange salary information. The exchange guarantees fair treatment to employees. Confidential and factual, it clears up erroneous salary notions that sometimes arise through rumor.

For general surveys, the compiling agency (either the company itself or a third party serving a number of companies) usually provides a form.

Restrictions

Salary data obtained from other employers are obviously confidential. That they often come from competitors makes them especially sensitive.

The value of salary survey data is of such overriding importance that precautions must be taken to ensure accuracy and comprehensiveness. Nothing must occur that would discourage full and frank participation. Accordingly, general surveys include measures to make sure that no participating firm will suffer from the release of the information that it provides. For example, salaries are identified by position, not by name of incumbent. If the survey is being conducted by a third party, position salaries are not identified with the corresponding participant company. Companies are code-named A, B, C, and so on—and the codes are known only to the neutral compiling agency.

The people working with the data are pledged to keep it confidential. It would be unethical, for example, for a salary administrator who happens to learn the identity of Company B on the survey report to disclose this to others in his or her company. From the salary data thus uncovered, they might be able to arrive at an estimate of a competitor's overhead costs.

OUTPUT DATA

What is obtained from a salary survey depends on who is conducting it. Typically, the output includes the following:

1. *A list of jobs covered by the survey together with brief job descriptions.* As mentioned earlier, the descriptions enable the user to match the survey jobs and salaries with those

Figure 12. Survey job descriptions.

SYSTEMS ANALYSIS

Manager or Supervisor of Systems Analysis (Job No. 10)
Plans, organizes, and controls activities of the systems analysis section in the establishment and implementation of new or revised systems and procedures. Usually considered as being *in full charge of all systems analysis activities*. Responsible for feasibility studies and systems design and makes recommendations on the action to be taken. Assigns personnel to the various projects and directs their activities. Consults with and advises other departments on systems and procedures.

Lead Systems Analyst (Job No. 11)
Often considered the *assistant manager of systems analysis*. Has full technical knowledge and also *has supervisory duties* of instructing, directing, and checking the work of the other systems analysts. *Assists in planning, organizing, and controlling the activities of the section.* Assists in scheduling the work of the section and assigning personnel to the various projects being studied or processed. May act for the manager in his absence.

Senior Systems Analyst (Job No. 12)
Under general direction, formulates logical statements of business problems and devises procedures for solutions of the problems. *Usually competent to work at the highest level of all technical phases of systems analysis* while working on his own most of the time. May give some direction and guidance to lower-level classifications. Confers with management to define the data processing problem. Analyzes existing system logic difficulties and revises the logic and procedures involved as required.

Junior Systems Analyst (Job No. 13)
Under direct supervision, *assists higher-level classifications* in devising computer system specifications and record layouts. Usually fairly competent to work on several phases of systems analysis with only general direction, but still *needs some instruction and guidance* for the other phases. Studies and analyzes existing office procedures as assigned. Prepares systems flow charts to describe existing and proposed operations. Prepares comprehensive computer block diagrams in accordance with instructions from higher-level classifications.

Reprinted from *Infosystems,* June 1978. Copyright Hitchcock Publishing Company.

in the user organization. Figure 12 shows several job descriptions from a survey by *Infosystems* magazine. These help to distinguish among various levels of the position described:

systems analyst. From them, the participating company can be sure that reported salaries agree with the type of work being done.

2. *The average salary, among the survey contributors, for each job.* This is frequently expressed as the median—the figure that falls midway in a ranking from lowest to highest.

Table 2 shows reported data from the *Infosystems* survey. Not only the median but other key salary levels are summarized, job by job. (Though not reproduced here, the *Infosystems* survey also provides job salary analysis by equipment rental costs, industry, and geographical area.) From the data you can learn, for example, that for junior computer systems analyst the modal (most frequent) salary is $307 a week and the median (midway) salary is $323.

3. *The range of salaries reported, from lowest to highest.* Table 3 excerpts data from a nationwide survey by the Bureau of Labor Statistics. From this tabulation you can learn, for example, that at a given time the monthly salaries of level II buyer (as defined in job descriptions that accompany the survey) range from $925 to $1,850, with an average of $1,350.

The BLS also publishes useful periodic surveys of position salaries in each standard metropolitan statistical area (SMSA). These publications can give you a rough idea of how salaries are running. They are worth referring to. You should, however, use them with care. For one thing, area differentials may influence the results. According to the BLS survey, "For most of the occupations, salary levels in metropolitan areas and in large establishments were higher than the average for all establishments within the full scope of the survey."

In addition, the national survey generally covers only establishments with over 100 (sometimes only over 250) workers. The area surveys do not include employers with fewer than 50 workers. You cannot tell from these surveys what small employers are paying. You know only what you are up

TABLE 2   *Weekly salaries for all*

	Top Official	Manager of Data Processing	Asst. Mgr. of Data Processing	Project/Team Leader	Mgr. or Supervisor of Computer Systems Analysis and Programming
Number Reported	531	1042	207	419	454
Lowest Reported					
Actual Salary	300	184	173	196	197
25th Percentile[a]					
Actual Salary	500	384	336	369	374
National Average					
Actual Salary	641	472	431	443	446
Median[b]					
Actual Salary	576	461	423	436	432
Mode[c]					
Actual Salary	576	461	423	365	346
75th Percentile[d]					
Actual Salary	730	538	500	490	507
Highest Reported					
Actual Salary	1923	1538	913	880	826
Established Salary					
Range—Average Low	521	452	558	351	376
Established Salary					
Range—Average High	740	638	811	496	529

[a] That point at which 25% of all other salaries are lower and 75% are higher.
[b] A figure having an equal number above and below.
[c] The salary reported most often.
[d] That point at which 75% of all other salaries are lower and 25% are higher.
Reprinted from *Infosystems*, June 1978. Copyright Hitchcock
Publishing Company.

Infosystems jobs, nationwide.

Lead Computer Systems Analyst and Programmer	Senior Computer Systems Analyst and Programmer	Junior Computer Systems Analyst and Programmer	Mgr. or Supervisor of Computer Systems Analysis	Lead Computer Systems Analyst	Senior Computer Systems Analyst	Junior Computer Systems Analyst	Mgr. or Supervisor of Programming
548	1162	824	89	114	367	185	111
185	161	161	288	269	196	175	192
331	307	244	423	368	346	285	346
398	359	288	482	428	386	329	406
380	350	286	480	423	386	323	400
346	288	288	423	423	346	307	480
458	403	326	550	461	423	370	470
812	620	540	700	607	576	519	709
331	297	251	403	350	311	268	358
460	413	354	559	474	441	373	486

TABLE 3   *Employment distribution by salary:*

Monthly Salary	Buyers			
	I	II	III	IV
Under $725	1.2	—	—	—
$725 and under $750	1.0	—	—	—
$750 and under $775	1.5	—	—	—
$775 and under $800	2.8	—	—	—
$800 and under $825	1.9	—	—	—
$825 and under $850	3.4	—	—	—
$850 and under $875	5.8	—	—	—
$875 and under $900	6.5	—	—	—
$900 and under $925	5.2	—	—	—
$925 and under $950	2.6	(2.8)	—	—
$950 and under $975	5.6	1.1	—	—
$975 and under $1,000	5.7	1.1	—	—
$1,000 and under $1,050	10.5	2.6	—	—
$1,050 and under $1,100	7.9	4.0	—	—
$1,100 and under $1,150	8.4	6.4	(1.8)	—
$1,150 and under $1,200	5.6	7.8	1.1	—
$1,200 and under $1,250	6.3	9.6	3.1	—
$1,250 and under $1,300	2.3	9.5	3.4	—
$1,300 and under $1,350	3.7	10.5	4.5	—
$1,350 and under $1,400	3.2	7.3	4.9	(1.7)
$1,400 and under $1,450	1.5	7.1	6.0	1.0
$1,450 and under $1,500	2.8	6.5	8.3	2.8

Note: To avoid showing small proportions of employees scattered at or near the extremes of the distributions for some occupations, the percentages of employees in these intervals have been accumulated and are shown in the interval above or below the extreme interval containing at least 1 percent. The percentages representing these employees are shown in parentheses. Because of rounding, sums of individual items may not equal 100.

against in the big competition for employees. Keep in mind, too, that the data will be a little out of date by the time you receive them. You will have to adjust them for changing economic conditions.

4. *A breakdown of the salaries that fall into subdivisions of the range.* For example, salaries may be grouped according to the first, second, third, and fourth quarters of the ranking, which are separated by "quartiles" or "percentiles." This

professional and administrative occupations—buyers.

	Buyers			
Monthly Salary	I	II	III	IV
$1,500 and under $1,550	1.3	5.6	8.0	2.8
$1,550 and under $1,600	1.0	4.7	7.2	2.8
$1,600 and under $1,650	(2.4)	2.9	9.0	4.2
$1,650 and under $1,700	—	2.1	6.6	4.9
$1,700 and under $1,750	—	2.1	6.8	5.7
$1,750 and under $1,800	—	1.7	5.2	6.5
$1,800 and under $1,850	—	(4.4)	5.9	6.1
$1,850 and under $1,900	—	—	3.2	7.3
$1,900 and under $1,950	—	—	2.9	6.2
$1,950 and under $2,000	—	—	3.1	5.1
$2,000 and under $2,050	—	—	1.4	3.7
$2,050 and under $2,100	—	—	1.6	5.6
$2,100 and under $2,150	—	—	1.7	4.2
$2,150 and under $2,200	—	—	1.0	4.5
$2,200 and under $2,250	—	—	1.0	4.5
$2,250 and under $2,300	—	—	(2.7)	2.8
$2,300 and under $2,350	—	—	—	2.6
$2,350 and under $2,400	—	—	—	2.4
$2,400 and under $2,450	—	—	—	2.3
$2,450 and under $2,500	—	—	—	1.6
$2,500 and over	—	—	—	8.8
Total	100.0	100.0	100.0	100.0
Number of employees	5,345	14,472	15,289	4,544
Average monthly salary	$1,074	$1,350	$1,632	$1,988

SOURCE: Bureau of Labor Statistics Bulletin 2004, "National Survey of Professional, Administrative, Technical, and Clerical Pay," March 1978.

gives you an idea of the amount of salary dispersion (see Table 2).

5. *An explanation of any associated information.* For example, it is important to know if the jobs listed are bonus or nonbonus jobs, since this affects salary level. Many other factors may also be essential to the evaluation of data: whether a car is given to salespeople, whether the reported salaries include cost-of-living allowances for certain locations, whether

the salaries are influenced by unions, and so on. Some companies give all their employees an annual increase on one date. How does this date relate to the survey data? (If it falls one month after the survey, that is a fact worth knowing.)

SALARY CURVE CONSTRUCTION

From survey data, properly analyzed, a survey salary curve can be constructed. This consists of a wage curve based on the surveyed salaries for as many of your positions as possible. This curve can be compared with the curve for your present standard salaries to see if there is a difference requiring an update.

Before constructing the curve, you must review the data carefully in order to select those positions in the survey that are equivalent to ones in your company. You can do this with as many jobs as possible, or you can limit it to the company's benchmark list, which has been established as being correctly evaluated.

Your next task is to select from the survey data those salaries that tally with your company policy. Thus, if company policy is to pay the average that other companies pay for similar work, the average survey salary for each position is used. But if the policy is to do better—"to meet the third quartile salary" of other employers, for example—the appropriate quartile figure is used.

You may also winnow out from the survey data any "wild" figures that are reported—superhigh salaries attributable to only a few individuals, for example. You should then match the reported salaries against your company-evaluated points for the corresponding positions.

From this analysis you can construct the survey salary curve. As shown in Figures 13 and 14, the curve can relate going salaries to the evaluated points or to the company grades into which the surveyed positions already fall. The dots on the graph are reported values, and the line is a fit that

Figure 13. Salary survey curve: evaluated points.

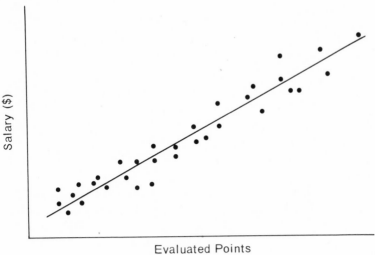

Evaluated Points

Figure 14. Salary survey curve: job grades.

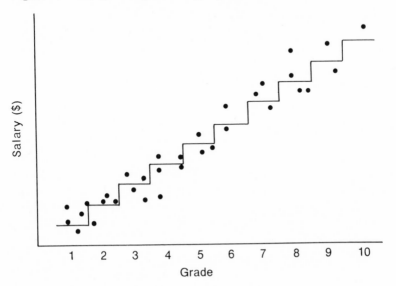

Grade

strikes an average. The data may be plotted as a single line or as steps.

As with the company salary curve, the survey curve may consist of several lines if your company is large enough to justify separate scales. In Figure 15, the "sales" line falls lower than the "managerial and professional" line because in the company the salespeople receive a bonus in addition to base salary, which may more than overcome the difference.

Survey Salary Curve

Juxtaposing the survey salary curve with the company salary curve shows whether the company's "official" salaries are in line with those of other employers. As an example, let us assume a single curve rather than the multiple curves shown in the preceding illustration (Figure 15). A comparison of survey with company salaries might appear as in Figure 16.

In looking at the graph, you should keep in mind that you

Figure 15. Salary survey curve: separate scales.

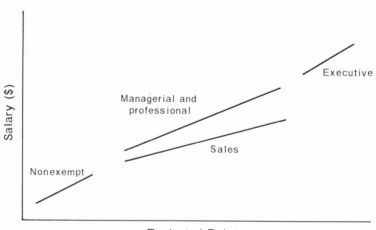

are dealing with a comparison between paid salaries outside and "standard" or "official" salaries inside. The outside values are salaries actually paid for positions at the time of the survey. T..e inside values—the company curve—are midpoints of ranges applicable to the positions in question; they are not necessarily actuals. Your purpose is to establish a company curve such that the midpoint of the ranges will correspond to the salaries paid elsewhere—that is, paid to that element of the employee universe with which you mean to maintain parity (or more or less than parity, depending on your policy).

Presumably, the survey data have just been received. The last comparison was made a year ago. In an inflationary period you may expect that your survey curve should be higher now than a year ago. In a noninflationary (but not deflationary) period, it should not change.

Figure 16. Survey salary curve versus company salary curve.

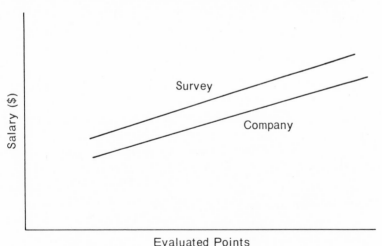

Adjustments to Company Curve

You now face the task of adjusting the existing company curve so that it will bear the proper relationship to the survey curve. To return to the example above, suppose that the survey is 6 percent higher than the company curve. You could adjust the company curve 6 percent to bring it in line. This would mean restating the midpoints so that each is 6 percent higher than before. For example:

	Midpoint Salary	
Grade	*Was*	*Is*
7	$1,000	$1,060
8	$1,100	$1,166
9	$1,210	$1,283
10	$1,330	$1,410

Would this bring you to a salary level comparable with that of the firms with which you wish to compete for employees? Not quite. Several additional factors must be taken into account.

When was the survey taken? What month is it now? Suppose (as is likely) it has taken three months to compile and distribute the survey data. By the time you analyze the data and make your new midpoints and ranges effective, another month will have passed.

What is the trend of the payroll economy? If it is upward, then other companies will be giving inflationary increases over the twelve months succeeding the survey data. As a result, if you set your midpoints equal to the survey data, they will be out of date as soon as you issue them. They will fall further behind as the survey year progresses.

For example, suppose the survey shows that among other companies the median salary for your benchmark job, inventory records clerk, was $1,200 as of May 1. You receive this information on September 1. By October 1 you have analyzed the results of the survey and are ready to install your new curve. Salary inflation is running at 6 percent a year. If on your new curve the midpoint for your inventory records clerk is $1,200, it will probably be a little behind the September averages of the surveyed companies. Some of their employees will have received increases in the interim. By the time next May rolls around, your curve will be even more behind the average. Therefore, your new curve must be set somewhat above the survey curve.

What effect all this has on your company's salaries depends on one more factor: Where do actual salaries stand in relation to the curve? Curve adjustments are discussed in more detail in the next chapter.

SHORTCUT

The salary curve procedures just described are a systematic way of keeping salary levels current. But are they the kind of thing that a small employer needs to deal with? Perhaps not. The basic principles are worth knowing, but if you don't have enough employees to warrant generalized treatment, you can shortcut the process.

Let's assume that you have a relatively small number of salaried positions. In the interests of order, equity, and control you have established standard salaries and ranges for each. Now your only problem is to keep these values up to date. To do so, you:

1. List your positions, with their ranges.
2. Obtain survey data on positions comparable to yours.
3. Determine by what percentage these data differ from those for the same survey positions a year ago.

4. Multiply your standard salaries by these percentages, and adjust the range max and mins to preserve the spread.

Instead of doing steps 2 and 3, you can find out from surveys the percentage by which other employers have adjusted their ranges since last year, without making a position-by-position comparison. Then go to step 4.

You now have a list of updated standard salaries, and because your adjustment is based on surveyed statistics, you can feel confident that you are keeping your policy abreast of competition. Keep in mind, however, that this shortcut suffices only if your firm has a small number of positions. If your position list is so long that a line-by-line approach is impossible, you should use the more general method of curve alignment.

PROBLEMS AND RISKS

In the words of the poet Alexander Pope:

> Some ne'er advance a judgment of their own,
> But catch the spreading notion of the Town.

In salary management, to catch the "spreading notion" of going pay levels is the purpose of salary surveys. No matter what your own judgment tells you is the *right* pay, you have to be guided by what other employers are doing. But merely ascertaining the facts about their practice is fraught with problems and risks.

Failure to Match Policy. Let us say that your company is situated in an inaccessible, inconvenient locality. To compensate for this, in the hopes of attracting desirable employees, the company adopts a policy of paying more than other companies competing for the same type of employee. Matching the salary curve exactly to survey averages may be an initial step toward violating the stated policy of paying more.

Misleading Titles. "Draftspeople at XYZ Company make half again as much as they do here. We aren't in line." But "draftspeople" (or "draftsmen") covers a multitude of skills. Perhaps the ones at XYZ are working on designs of new machines and yours are recording the piping layouts in the factory. You can't assume that the title tells you what the job is. Some brief job description must be referred to.

A good example of an uninformative title is "factory manager." Your survey should provide salary data only on managers running factories of roughly the same size and complexity as yours. And how far do their responsibilities extend? Do they handle their own purchasing, engineering design, accounting, inventory control, warehousing, and customer service? Or are these handled by headquarters? Titles alone do not tell the story.

Inadequate Sample. Your survey, a sample of the competitive universe, should represent that universe. No use surveying only the small companies in your neighborhood if there is a giant employer influencing salary levels. No use surveying the giants and missing the local discount store. And if you have a salaried union (in place or knocking at the door), it may be conducting its own survey.

Inappropriate Sample. Your sample should, insofar as possible, compare with the group from which you expect to draw (or to which you might lose) employees. If you are in the textile industry, for example, you don't need aerospace engineers in your survey group. If the nearest big city is 60 miles away, you may not wish to include nonexempt salaries from that area. Many companies prefer to survey their own locality for nonexempt positions, and their own industry for exempt positions, in order to get a fair comparison.

Diverse Nonsalary Payments. Some companies pay a bonus in addition to salary; others say that the salary should fully compensate for the employee's efforts without icing the cake with a bonus. Some companies pay a cost-of-living allowance separate from base pay; others absorb it in salary. Some companies provide free meals, uniforms, bus service, parking, clinical service, and a host of other fringes; others do not. Trained salary administrators know how to take such differences into account in using survey data. Other employees, including supervisors who may make informal surveys, do not always do so. As a result, they may feel that their own company's salary structure is too high or too low.

Economic Changes. When the rate of inflation is changing rapidly, survey data, being essentially past data, may be an inadequate guide for positioning a salary curve that is to be effective for the next twelve months. It may be necessary to survey more frequently in order to keep abreast of trends. Salary administrators in most companies rely both on formal outside services and on informal contacts with their counterparts in other companies to get a feel for what is happening.

Out-of-Line Occupations. From time to time the demand for a specific occupation outstrips the current supply. For example, there have been times when systems analysts, chemical engineers, programmers, and business planners have been in such demand that competition raised their salaries above what an objective skills evaluation might dictate. In a survey such positions should be handled separately. Their relatively high remuneration should not average up the salary curve for all positions. On the other hand, knowing the going salary for these jobs is essential if you are to attract and retain desirable employees.

Actuals Versus Ranges. "Something's wrong with our salary structure. We've lost three good employees who found they could make more money somewhere else." This statement may be an indictment not so much of the salary structure as of the actual salaries being paid. Were the employees already at the top of their range? Had they been getting regular increases? Could they have received more pay within the existing structure? Was salary, in fact, the problem? Salary is often given as the up-front reason for a move that was initiated by other, unstated dissatisfactions.

Prior to retirement, **Stanley B. Henrici** was General Manager of Organization Systems for Heinz, U.S.A., in Pittsburgh. A frequent contributor to business publications, he is also the author of STANDARD COSTS FOR MANUFACTURING (3rd edition), published by McGraw-Hill.

7: COMPARATIO

In a large sense, salary administration has two chief objectives:

1. To establish available salary levels (or ranges) that bear a predetermined relationship to the salaries paid by other employers. These levels, based on surveys, constitute your salary curve.
2. To see that the actual salaries being paid in your company conform to these levels.

Unless objective 2 is satisfied, the actual salaries paid will not bear the desired relationship to external salaries. Consider the following scenarios:

Company A

PRESIDENT OF COMPANY: Smith, we seem to be losing a good many of our technical people to other companies. Are you sure our salaries are competitive?

PERSONNEL MANAGER: Oh, no question about it. Our salary ranges are right in line.

PRESIDENT: Well, maybe you ought to check a few other companies, just to be sure.

PERSONNEL MANAGER: But I have. We just completed our annual survey, and job for job we are comparable with anyone else in our industry. In fact, the maximums of our ranges are slightly above the top salaries being paid by others. We can pay just as much as they do.

Company B

PRESIDENT OF COMPANY: Jones, we've been comparing our general administrative overhead with the financial statements of other companies in our industry. We're high. Now, I've done a little digging, and I find we don't have any more people per sales dollar than they do, so we must be paying more. Have you let us get into the position of being the highest-pay company in our field?

PERSONNEL MANAGER: No way! I have actual survey data from other companies. Our salary ranges, job for job, are no higher than theirs. Here, I'll show them to you. Look at the average salary for general accountants in companies D, E, F, and G. In every case the salary is more than our midpoint.

Something is wrong here, of course. What's wrong is that the president is talking about actual salaries paid, while the personnel manager is referring to the salary ranges—not what *is* paid but what can be paid. Apples and oranges.

In both scenarios the salary ranges agreed with competitors' pay, but apparently the actual salaries within the company did not. This difference led to problems. It is therefore important to have some measure of actual versus standard salaries. In this chapter we will examine the correlation between the salary ranges on your pay curve and the actual salaries on your payroll.

COMPARATIO DEFINED

The *comparatio* is a common and important measure of company salary status. It is computed as follows:

$$\text{Comparatio} = \frac{\text{actual salaries}}{\text{standard (midpoint, or basic) salaries}}$$

TABLE 4
Data for computing comparatio.

Grade	Standard Midpoint Salary	No. of People	Average Actual Salary
1	$ 600	20	$ 550
2	700	9	650
3	800	9	750
4	900	6	800
5	1,000	5	1,050
6	1,200	4	1,300
7	1,500	3	1,700
8	1,900	1	2,300
9	2,400	0	—
10	2,900	1	2,800

For example, suppose that the ten salary grades in your company, the number of people, average salary, and standard midpoint salaries are as shown in Table 4. From the data it can be calculated that the weighted average actual salary for the whole company is $846. If all employees were being paid at the standard salary (or midpoint) of the respective range for their positions, the average salary would be $862. The comparatio, then, is $846/$862 = .98. If the weighted actual average salary were $900, the comparatio would be $900/$862 = 1.04.

When no grades are used, the comparatio is equal to the sum of the actual salaries divided by the sum of the standard salaries for the corresponding positions.

Specific Comparatios

A comparatio may also be calculated for a given grade or group of grades. In our example, the comparatio for grade 1 is the average actual salary for that grade divided by the standard salary, or $550/$600 = .92. If the first three grades consist mostly of nonexempt employees hired from the local area, you may wish to know the comparatio for that group. It is $621/$671 = .93.

In fact, the ratio may be calculated for specific occupations. You might, for example, figure the comparatio of your supervisory force, which comprises a subset of employees in several grades. To do so you would use the average actual and standard salaries of those supervisors. You might look at the comparatios of females versus males, blacks versus whites, or oldsters versus youngsters to see if a bias exists. To an outsider, a low comparatio for a protected group may look like discrimination.

Significance of Comparatio

What the comparatio tells you is, of course, how closely your actual salaries approximate the basic salaries, or midpoints, of your salary curve. Theoretically, then, it should also tell you how close your actual salaries come to the surveyed salaries of other companies from which your curve was derived. But this depends, in turn, on two other factors: (1) your policy regarding competitiveness and (2) how long ago the surveyed salaries were effective.

For the first point, you may have decided that you want to pay 10 percent more than the average of other companies. You set your salary curve 10 percent higher than survey results. If your current comparatio is 1.00, then your average actual salaries are equivalent to your salary curve midpoints, and hence are 10 percent over surveyed employers. You are in fact doing as you intended—provided that you consider the second factor.

The second factor is one of timing. Suppose the salary curve reflects survey data obtained eight months ago, without adjustment for the time lapse. In the interim the surveyed companies may have raised their salary level. With a current comparatio of 1.00, you are not relating to the outside world as you intended.

Even an employer with only ten salaried employees should check the ratio of actual to standard salaries. The comparatio tells if salary rates are running ahead of or behind planned levels.

SALARY CURVE ADJUSTMENT

Salary curves must be set so that they will be realistic over some future period, usually a year. (In dynamic inflationary periods, some companies review their curves more often than annually.) In a noninflationary period, such as we assumed in Chapter 4, the curve remains unchanged from one year to the next. That is, the average pay for an array of specific positions in a substantial universe of companies is stationary. Throughout a period of rising salaries, on the other hand, each year's curve is higher than the last. Accordingly, as you obtain survey information, you must make a decision: By how much must your curve go up?

Now things get complicated.

First, you must look at your policy. If it is to pay more (or less) than other companies offer, you must multiply your survey curve by whatever percentage is necessary to achieve that end. Then you must consider timing. Outside salary levels have probably inflated since the survey. By the time another survey rolls around they will be still higher. Where should you place your curve so that you will be in line with your policy by that time?

This is an area that obviously calls for judgment. One simple solution is to adjust the curve by the same percentage as that by which the survey data changed. If the survey levels have gone up 5 percent since the previous rollcall, you raise your own curve 5 percent. This is all right if you were more or less in line to begin with.

If, however, your curve is noticeably out of line with the others, you will want to adjust for this as well. You can do so by following this procedure:

1. Draw your existing curve and the survey curve on a graph, as illustrated in Figure 17.

2. Estimate the likely upward movement between the date of the survey and the present date. If you believe that the salary market has been recently going up at 6 percent a year and the survey was taken four months ago, the change is $4/12 \times 6\% = 2\%$.

3. Add the 2 percent to your survey data and draw a corrected, "current" survey curve on your graph, as shown in Figure 18. This is where you think surveyed salaries could be today.

4. Assuming that your 6 percent trend will hold for another twelve months, the survey data a year from now should be about 6 percent higher than your corrected, "current" curve. Midway through a year, a survey would theoretically come out 3 percent higher than today. Draw on your graph a curve 3 percent higher than the "current" curve, as shown in Figure 19. This is your new standard salary curve. For the next six months you will presumably experience a comparatio below 1.00, and for the following six months, as salary increases accumulate, you will experience a comparatio over 1.00. Then you will resurvey and readjust.

Again, all this calls for considerable judgment. It involves estimates and averages. For one thing, your new salary curve is "true" only at the next midyear point. As a result, when you scan your comparatio each month, you must keep in mind what month it is. Therefore, you may wish to consider a further refinement: use the "current" survey curve as your standard curve in the first month and program your computer to index it upward each succeeding month. Then your standard curve will always be in sync—provided your esti-

Figure 17. Original survey curve.

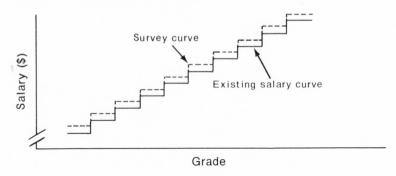

Figure 18. Corrected "current" survey curve.

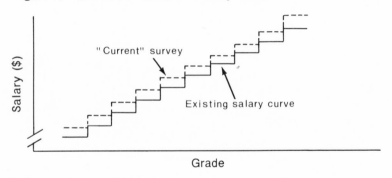

Figure 19. New salary curve.

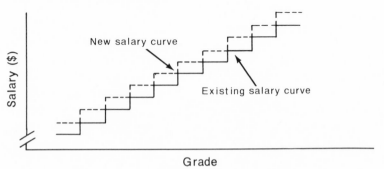

mates were correct. Theoretically, your comparatio will hold at 1.00.

SALARY LEVEL COMPONENTS

As noted earlier, your ability to maintain salary levels that are fair both to employees and to the company depends on your salary policy, as expressed in the height and range of the salary curve, and on the amount and frequency of salary increases and level of hiring rates. The comparatio measures the degree to which actual salaries paid average out with the policy curve.

The point to remember is that adjusting the curve and its ranges upward does not in itself change actual salaries being paid. The actual salaries advance only when you give a corresponding "range adjustment" increase. This increase holds your employees at par with changes in the economy. It also holds them steady at their position in the range. (Only an additional merit increase will move them up in the range.)

The comparatio is the compass that tells you whether you are moving toward your destination: the policy. If the comparatio for the entire salary payroll is less than 1.00, you are paying low. If it is greater than 1.00, you are paying high. For either of these conditions there are usually explanations. On simplified graphs we can compare the high and low comparatio effects.

In a company that was on the average paying all its employees 5 percent less than the midpoint, the comparatio would be .95. A graph of the company's actual versus policy salary curves is shown in Figure 20. By contrast, a company averaging 5 percent over midpoint in all grades would have a comparatio of 1.05. Its graph is shown in Figure 21.

Within a given range, the dispersion of actual salaries determines the comparatio for that range, as shown in Figure 22. Each dot represents an individual salary.

Figure 20. Actual versus policy salaries: low comparatio.

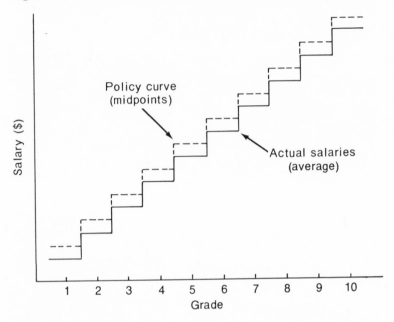

LOW COMPARATIO

A low comparatio suggests any one of several conditions.

Rapid Turnover. A relatively large number of people are leaving your company and being replaced by newcomers. Few employees stay around long enough to rise high in the salary ranges. This situation may raise questions. If people are leaving voluntarily, why? Is your company unsatisfactory as a place to work? After all, people apparently thought the hiring salary made it worth joining to begin with. If employees are leaving involuntarily, again why? Are you consistently hiring people who can't meet job demands and who have to be replaced? What is this costing you?

Figure 21. Actual versus policy salaries: high comparatio.

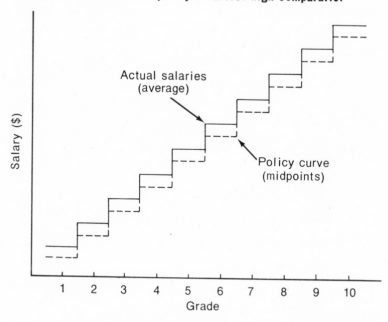

Figure 22. Salary dispersion in range for various comparatios.

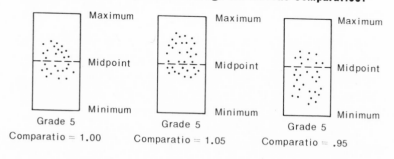

Lagging Salary Growth. Your salary increases are not large enough or frequent enough to move employees up through the ranges. For example, you move the curve up 8 percent to stay abreast of the job market. But your employees average an increase of only 5 percent. Your average salaries, and your comparatio, are falling behind. This lag may reflect a deliberate short-term thrust to hold down salary expense under adversity. If so, it may meet its objective at the cost of losing some employees to companies offering better pay. On the other hand, it may occur merely because you didn't adjust your salary increase guidelines to match the salary curve change. Still again, it may result from the zeal of a salary administrator or manager who hates to approve increases because "it's just too much money." A few company scrooges can subvert any policy, always with the best of intentions.

Aging Workforce. A large block of employees who joined your company during an expansion long ago have all reached retirement age more or less simultaneously. As these higher-salaried workers leave, they are replaced by newcomers or "promotees" who start low in the ranges for the jobs in question. This not uncommon event causes a temporary depression in the comparatio.

Unrealistic Policy. The comparatio is low only because your policy curve is too high. Though you have a policy of "paying 15 percent better than the market," you have been able to attract and retain an okay group of people for something less. Perhaps the policy should be reexamined.

Substandard Workforce. Your low comparatio shows that you are indeed paying less than standard and less than other employers. What does this say about the caliber of your workforce—people who are willing to work for relatively low pay? Are your productivity, sales, customer relations, and general efficiency suffering? Or do you have managers so brilliant that they can keep the works running with marginal employees? If so, a low comparatio may be just what you are looking for.

Sudden Expansion. Your company has been growing rapidly. You have hired many new employees at competitive starting rates, in accordance with your policy. But because they are new, they are in the lower part of their ranges. Their presence in the population pulls the average comparatio down.

Time of Year. Your comparatio is lower than 1.00 because you are looking at it in the early months of the year, before salary increases have moved average actual salaries up to the standard curve.

HIGH COMPARATIO

A comparatio greater than 1.00 suggests that you have an average salary level higher than you intended. Several factors may cause such a condition.

Stability of Population. In any given year, you would expect a number of older employees to retire or resign and to be replaced by new ones. The loss of people high in their ranges and the acquisition of newcomers low in the ranges would keep the comparatio floating close to your policy curve—close to the midpoint salaries. But if few people are leaving, your whole employee population is moving up through the ranges via merit increases. Short of firing the most senior employees or putting a cap on merit increases, you will have to live with this situation. But it does raise an interesting question: Is your turnover *too* low? Unless you do something, your salary average is going to be higher than that of other employers for comparable jobs.

Excessive Merit Increases. Your supervisors and managers hate to think that their own employees, whom they have trained so well that they can rely on them utterly, are merely "satisfactory" or "competent." Accordingly, they give them all high merit ratings and correspondingly high merit increases. Up goes the comparatio.

Sudden Expansion. A rapid growth in the workforce can raise (as well as lower) the comparatio: it all depends on what kind of people you hire. As stated earlier, an influx of new employees at starting, or minimum, salaries depresses the ratio. But what if you can't make it with novices? You need people who are already up to speed, with all wheels turning when they arrive in your company. So you have to lure them from other employers by paying them higher salaries than they already receive. When you do, your comparatio is going to rise. This upcreep also implies an elevation of your overhead costs compared with that of the competitors from whom you hired those essential people. And now that you have these high-priced stars, you will have to keep on giving them increases in the future. Your salaries, swelling above the midpoint, yield a high comparatio.

Sudden Contraction. Business is off or your net profit is not where the bankers and analysts think it should be. So your company sets in motion a cutback, a "ruthless assault on insupportable levels of overhead." Deadwood and substandard performers are to be excised from the payroll. In your case, you decide that this means getting rid of newer employees. You hold on to the older ones because of their experience and EEO shelter. What is the result? You end up with a preponderance of people in the upper end of their salary ranges. Your comparatio drifts up a few notches.

Time of Year. It is almost a year since your last competitive survey and curve overhaul. In the interim you have been giving both merit and inflationary salary increases. Even if your comparatio was 1.00 at some point in the year, it will be more now. Salaries both in your company and in everyone else's are escalating upward. So it is perfectly understandable that your comparatio has climbed. When you adjust your salary curve to reflect current market conditions, the midpoints will be higher and your comparatio correspondingly less.

SUBSETS

From the foregoing sections it can be seen that the comparatio provides valuable insights into a company's actual payment practice as compared with what it thinks is its policy.

The same analysis can be made of subsets—divisions, departments, or even individual occupations within the company. For example, Department A has a comparatio of .85 and Department B one of 1.20. Why the difference? Is the head of Department A holding back on increases because of budget problems? Should the employees there—who after all are company employees, not Department A employees—suffer because their department overspent on raw materials?

And what about Department B? According to the department head, the employees there are all so superior that they have been getting above-average increases for the last three years. "Good motivation—look at the results." Look at our payroll, you say. An elite corps!

And here is Department C, running a comparatio of 1.35. Why is this? Oh, Department C is the process design department. If you want to catch and hold chemical engineers, you have to pay the going salaries, and they're high. You can't derive them from a salary curve made up of the average of many different positions.

Still another department may have a low comparatio because most of its employees are newcomers. Yet another may have a high one because it is staffed with unpromotable old-timers.

All the factors that influence comparatio at the company level also operate within the subsets of the organization. To try to force all subsets to the same level would probably be a mistake. Nonetheless, examination of internal comparatios may disclose opportunities for improvement. Specifically, it may lead to questions such as the following:

1. Are supervisors operating on their own, rather than according to company policy?
2. Are there groups of high-in-the-range employees who should be considered for promotion?
3. Are there areas where a low comparatio signals possible pay dissatisfaction, an entry point for unions?
4. Are there areas where a low comparatio suggests an excessive number of new employees, possibly in need of training?
5. If a high comparatio in an area means that you are paying more than the going rates, what is the effect on costs? Why, in fact, *are* you paying more?

PROBLEMS AND RISKS

Figuring the comparatio is no great task, especially when salary data are deposited in a computer. It is in the actions taken as a result of this statistic that difficulties may arise.

Change in General Salary Practice. Your company finds that its comparatio is low. A decision is made to raise it by means of a general increase in salaries. But perhaps the real question is: Is the policy curve wrong? If your seemingly low salary level presents no difficulties in hiring or holding on to employees, what you are paying may be about right. What the low comparatio suggests is that you have an unrealistically high policy curve—at least at this point in your review cycle.

Conversely, if your company's comparatio is high, you cannot jump to the conclusion that you should slow down on increases until it gets back in line. Why is it high? Is it possible that standard salaries are running behind the market? Maybe it is the policy curve that needs changing.

Inaction. If you fail to raise the policy curve when surveys indicate that you should, you risk losing or demotivating better or more senior employees. They are the ones most likely to be near the range maximums. Unless the ranges are raised when they should be, these employees will run out of space for increases. If inflation exists, they will begin to feel pinched. A high comparatio signals that a majority of your employees are in the upper ends of the range, with no salary growth ahead of them.

Global Conclusions. A look at the comparatio for the company as a whole may suggest that all is well. But beneath the surface there may be pockets of potential trouble. Suppose that the overall company ratio is 1.00—right on the button— but in one department it is only .80. What does this mean? If the department is full of junior employees who came in at the starting rate, well and good. If not, you may ask if this group should in fact be running behind the company average.

Trend Checking. Since the standard curve remains constant throughout the year, between revisions it can serve as a baseline for checking trends in the actual salary level. Normally, merit and range adjustment increases, if granted throughout the year, gradually elevate the actual salary average. By periodically checking the comparatio, you can determine if this escalation is moving at the anticipated rate. Theoretically, the ratio should be somewhat less than 1.00 immediately after range adjustment. By the time the next survey occurs, it should have moved to a value greater than 1.00.

Checking the ratio trend for subsidiaries of a conglomerate, for divisions of a company, for departments of a division, or even for types of occupations permits an assessment of relative salary movement. Unless this is done, the company has no assurance that its stated policies are being observed.

Sudden Changes. In addition to watching your comparatio, you may find it advisable to keep an eye on the external climate. Sudden changes—up or down—have been known to occur in the salary market. These may be caused by a recession, a boom, inflation, or the imposition or relaxation of controls. When such a change occurs, your first step is to bring the policy curve in line with the environment. This will throw your comparatio out of line. Your next step is to adjust salary increases so that the comparatio will slide back to its intended position.

Guideline Adjustment. Salary increase guidelines should always be reviewed after the policy curve has been adjusted. The question is: Should they be tightened or loosened so that actual salary changes throughout the year will develop the comparatio that is desired?

8: APPRAISALS

WE HAVE SEEN how individual salaries may be distributed throughout a salary range, with some employees being near the minimum, others nearer the midpoint, and some approaching the maximum. From a company standpoint it is the location of these salaries that determines the comparatio. But what, in turn, determines this location? How does an employee move upward in the range?

The answer of course is through merit increases. Then what determines the amount, if any, of merit increases? The answer to this question, most of the time, is employee appraisal. Appraisal of the employee's qualifications or performance. Appraisal performed by the employee's supervisor.

Appraisal is the answer "most of the time" because in some companies merit increases, so-called, arrive automatically at periodic intervals. They acknowledge increasing job tenure or seniority. Yet even here a form of appraisal is implicit: whether or not the employee remains with the company long enough to get a tenure increase depends on the supervisor's appraisal. The supervisor, by keeping the employee on the payroll, is saying that performance justifies retention and hence justifies the increase that is forthcoming.

An appraisal, then, formal or otherwise, precedes the granting of a merit increase. The appraisal also shapes the nature of the increase—its occurrence, its size, and its timing. Appraisals are an essential part of a salary program.

NOMENCLATURE

Just to keep things straight, we should observe certain distinctions in nomenclature. A number of words have certain conventional meanings to those in the salary industry.

Evaluation. This term commonly refers to the determination of the level of a *position*. An evaluation is made of the characteristics and demands of a job, regardless of who the incumbent is. Evaluations are usually performed by a specialist or by a committee.

Appraisal. This term commonly refers to the determination of the skill, performance, ability, qualifications, or potential of an *individual*. It is performed by the employee's supervisor.

Assessment. This word sometimes crops up in the rating of employees, most frequently in the expression "assessment centers." The term refers to sessions in which, by means of interviews and possibly role tests, a group of superiors judges an employee's potential for future managerial positions. Proponents of the practice assert that such centers provide insight into an individual's future managerial performance. Opponents think that they provide insight only into an individual's ability to perform before an assessment center group.

NEED FOR FORMALITY

Why, it may be asked, make a big thing out of performance appraisal? How well people are performing is no secret. If they do satisfactory work, they know it. If they fall down on the job, they are told soon enough. Their boss is in touch with them every day. It's a waste of time, and embarrassing too, to make an annual ceremony out of what should be perfectly obvious.

The fact is employees often do not know how well they are doing—on the whole. Maybe one day they make an error, and another day they turn out a good piece of work. What does it all add up to? Even in the small, closely knit firm, employees have the same concerns as those in a large corporation: "How am I doing? Where am I headed?" They can't judge from the brief comments they hear every day, shaped by the boss's changing moods. They need a formal discussion.

Why formal? Because formality—the use of forms, in fact, to ensure coverage, communication, and recording of the message—is the best way to guarantee that the appraisal is made and that the employee knows it is being made. In addition, it helps you in deciding on and subsequently explaining the salary actions that you take.

PURPOSES OF APPRAISAL

Periodic appraisal of an employee's performance may serve a number of purposes:

1. To ascertain qualifications for an increase in salary.
2. To provide a basis for determining the amount and timing of an increase.
3. To rank the employee against all others in a department, grade, company, or type of work.
4. To record the employee's developmental history.
5. To identify a backlog of employees qualified to fill vacancies.
6. To determine the availability and readiness of the employee for transfer or promotion.
7. To satisfy the employee's desire to know how his or her supervisor regards the employee's progress and performance.
8. To make sure the employee is aware of and performing all requirements and duties of the job.
9. To determine whether previously set goals or objectives have been fulfilled.

10. To review the job description for accuracy.
11. To highlight areas in which the employee can improve performance on the job.
12. To discover areas in which the employee can train or develop in order to fill future jobs, as part of career planning.
13. To warn the employee of the need for improvement in performance or behavior.
14. To discover the need for training programs for numbers of employees who have a common deficiency.
15. To determine whether procedures and systems need to be improved in order to obtain better performance.
16. To provide feedback to help the supervisor improve his or her proficiency in management; or to improve departmental performance.
17. To detect symptoms of general dissatisfaction, unfavorable employee attitudes, unfavorable company image, or misunderstood or misapplied company policies.
18. To uncover situations where an employee is thinking of leaving the company.
19. To establish a record in case of future legal action by an employee.

TYPES OF APPRAISAL

After this imposing list of good purposes it must nevertheless be recognized that how an appraisal is best performed is by no means an agreed-on matter. In fact, whether an appraisal has any real meaning at all is debatable. In the personnel, psychological, and behavioral fields, there are varying views.

Those who condemn the process usually focus on its lack of objectivity. Appraisals, they say, are subject to the fancies of the appraiser. It is difficult to prove that they really relate to job requirements. They are inconsistent from one appraiser to another. They are tainted with opportunities for discrimination against minorities. They introduce considerations unrelated to actual performance of position duties.

Those who endorse appraisal focus on its necessity. They argue that since *some* form of judgment must be applied in deciding on raises and promotions, a formal, guided system with records is better than catch-as-catch-can guesswork. Not appraisals themselves but faulty methods of appraisal are to be criticized.*

One result of this diversity of opinion is a diversity of appraisal methods. Some of the common appraisal techniques are described below.

Checklist. For each employee the supervisor checks one of several levels indicating the overall rating. Some of the terms commonly used for the various levels are:

Distinguished, far exceeds requirements, outstanding, exceptional

Highly satisfactory, exceeds requirements, superior, good, highly effective

Satisfactory, meets requirements, average, competent, acceptable, effective

Marginal, meets some requirements, meets minimum, needs improvement, conditional

Unsatisfactory, fails to meet requirements, below minimum, inadequate

When a checklist is used, terms should be defined. For example, "superior" to whom or to what? To the normal job

---

* The subject is excellently covered in Conference Board Report 723, "Appraising Managerial Performance" (New York: The Conference Board, 1977).

requirements? To other employees in the company performing similar work? To employees performing similar work everywhere?

Critical Incident. The supervisor cites examples of what the employee has done. These are intended to illustrate the employee's performance on various job factors and thus to demonstrate performance through fact rather than opinion.

Objectives. When "management by objectives" is in force, the appraisal consists of a determination of how well the employee has met previously established goals or objectives. If the goals were quantitative, a numerical appraisal may be made.

Traits and Characteristics. The supervisor rates the employee on various traits deemed relevant to performance. A sample form is shown in Figure 23. The form is similar to the simple checklist but is expanded to cover personal as well as performance characteristics. One characteristic, not quite a trait, that is sometimes included is "promotability." Because this type of appraisal is difficult to validate, it may be vulnerable if put to an EEOC challenge.

Essay. The supervisor writes an essay describing the employee's behavior, performance, skills, deficiencies, accomplishments, failures, and so on.

Ranking. The supervisor ranks all employees from top to bottom according to proficiency. This approach does not seem unreasonable. However, think how a union might react to a ranking based on a supervisor's subjective impressions!

Forced Distribution. The supervisor assigns each employee to one of, say, five sections of an appraisal bell curve, based

Figure 23. Performance appraisal form.

Name_____ **INSTRUCTIONS** Location and Dept._____

Position Title_____ Date _____

(1) The employee should be reviewed on each of the factors below
in relation to the present position. For each of these factors,
check the box which reflects most typically the employee's
performance.

(2) Some factors are particularly significant in certain positions.
Circle the three factors which are *particularly important in
reviewing an employee in this position.*

Group	Factor Number	Factor	Low 1	2	3	4	High 5
Position Performance	1	Position knowledge	☐	☐	☐	☐	☐
	2	Analytical ability and judgment	☐	☐	☐	☐	☐
	3	Planning and execution	☐	☐	☐	☐	☐
	4	Acceptance of responsibility	☐	☐	☐	☐	☐
	5	Dependability	☐	☐	☐	☐	☐
	6	Creative thinking	☐	☐	☐	☐	☐
Personal Performance	7	Relationship with others	☐	☐	☐	☐	☐
	8	Attitude	☐	☐	☐	☐	☐
	9	Emotional stability	☐	☐	☐	☐	☐
	10	Health	☐	☐	☐	☐	☐
Supervisory Performance	11	Delegation of responsibility and authority	☐	☐	☐	☐	☐
	12	Personnel handling, leadership, and development	☐	☐	☐	☐	☐

SOURCE: Conference Board Report 723, "Appraising Managerial Performance"
(New York: The Conference Board, 1977).

on the assumption that such a curve should represent a group's distribution of characteristics. For example:

| | Permissible Percentage |
Rating	Receiving Rating
Superior	5%
Highly satisfactory	10
Satisfactory	70
Marginal	10
Unsatisfactory	5

This smacks a little of a quota system, to which unions have been known to object.

Job Description. The supervisor gauges the employee's performance against each duty or responsibility listed on the job description.

These methods are not mutually exclusive. Trait review, for example, can be combined with forced distribution. Often, the checklist is appended as a sort of summary to another form of appraisal.

The thoroughness of any appraisal system may vary from company to company. And its application may vary from supervisor to supervisor. Thus an appraisal may be merely a quickie snapshot of where the employee stands today—perhaps in relation to expectations or to the status of others. Or it may be an in-depth review of past progress and accomplishments, present assets and deficiencies, and developmental plans and goals for the future.

PARTICIPATION

In some companies the supervisor alone performs the appraisal. In others, he or she performs it jointly with the employee. Sometimes the employee first fills out a self-appraisal form as a basis for discussion. Nearly always the appraisal is reviewed by the next-higher level of management. Some employers provide an appeals system for employees who feel they did not get a fair review.

Generally, it is a good idea to have the employee participate. Certainly the employee should at least be informed of the results.

APPRAISAL AND MERIT INCREASES

As mentioned in an earlier chapter, merit increases within a company may vary from one individual to another. They may vary in both frequency and amount. What determines, for any employee, how often and how much? In a small, informal organization, both timing and amount may be tailored to the individual. The boss decides to give an employee a raise of so many dollars because the employee:

Has been pestering the boss for it.
Is a relative.
Is obviously in need of more earnings to meet personal demands.
Is personally loyal.
Is being wooed by another employer.
Has been doing good work.
Has passed through a probationary period.
Is being prepared for a higher position.
Is out of line in salary, compared with other employees.

In small enterprises where the owner is in touch with most of the employees, any of these reasons is valid—provided the boss and the employee think it is valid. (How it seems to other employees is another question.)

In a larger company where a number of supervisors can

grant increases, some of these reasons lose their validity. The welfare of the organization demands that salary increases relate to impartial and objective rules. One such rule is that the awarding of a merit increase must depend on the results of a written employee appraisal.

Thus, although employee appraisals have many purposes, their use as a foundation for merit increases is paramount. And since their outcome is reflected in dollars of income to the employee and cost to the employer, it is essential that they be executed uniformly and well.

This link between appraisals and salary has an important effect on employee morale. Employees who receive glowingly positive appraisals but only minimum salary increases will feel that they are being swindled or conned. Those who receive mediocre appraisals but (possibly placatory) large salary increases will lack motivation for improvement.

TIMING OF APPRAISALS

The timing of appraisals varies among firms. Some firms perform appraisals for all employees at one time—say, in the same week every year. An advantage of this system is that the appraisers can compare the performance of various individuals. They are "thinking appraisal," and by concentrating on it they will do a better job. When ranking or normal distribution systems are used, simultaneous appraisal is almost mandatory.

Other firms appraise each employee on his or her anniversary of employment. This practice allows more time to be spent with each individual. It can be more personalized than an appraisal that is part of a mass review. Still other firms appraise performance only when an employee is due for an increase.

Some firms perform a review when a person is transferred in order to establish a record of the employee's accomplishments on the job on which experience was acquired. Conceivably, ingoing performance on the new job will be below par for some time. Fairness requires a record that gives a complete picture.

In some companies the appraisal process is separated into two segments: overall appraisal and appraisal for salary change. Here the thinking is that discussions of employee performance, betterment, and career improvement should not be defiled by mercenary considerations of income. Improvement should be sought for its own sake, not for the prospect of monetary gain. This approach may sound a little idealistic, if not foolish. However, in a financially strapped company that has little to dole out for increases, there may be some sense in it.

Such a practice runs into trouble when an appraisal of general performance differs from appraisal for salary purposes. Suppose, for example, that Clara is rated "superior" in overall performance, but six months later gets a salary increase at the "average" level. Such an event might occur if the company has imposed a quota of 10 percent on increases rated at the "superior" level—and the quota has been reached by the time Clara's salary is reviewed. Clara will not understand this at all.

This is a point worth remembering when appraisals are all conducted at the same time. If salary increases are scattered throughout the year—and no remarkable interim changes in performance have occurred—the increases should more or less agree with those appraisals.

EFFECT OF APPRAISALS

Employees receiving "high" appraisals may get an increase sooner or greater (or both) than those receiving "average" ones. Thus appraisals affect how quickly employees move upward through the salary ranges.

A company that has a high comparatio might take a look at its supervisors' appraisals of employees. The high comparatio may be due simply to tenure and low turnover. But it may also disclose a tendency to overappraise. Too many stars. Excessively low standards and expectations.

This analysis may be carried into departments. Suppose a department has a low comparatio, caused by a group of uniformly low appraisals that resulted in few or minimum increases. Does this disclose an overly demanding supervisor, or has some unseen selective process loaded this department with mediocre workers?

TRAINING AND EDUCATION

Appraisals for salary purposes are valuable both to the company and to its employees. To the company they are important because of their effect on payroll costs as well as on turnover, morale, and employee development. To the employee they are obviously important because of their effect on income.

For these reasons the appraisal process cannot be taken for granted. Something is wrong if:

- There is a preponderance of ratings in the better-than-average category. This condition raises company costs. It also carries too many employees too rapidly toward the maximum of the range—which is, by definition, higher than surveyed averages. Once large numbers of employees are near the top, there is pressure to carry them beyond in order not to stop the accustomed pattern of increases. More cost.
- In a large group of employees—say, a major department—no one is appraised as superior. Too much consistency is unnatural.

- The high ratings are concentrated in the upper managerial levels, with none down the ranks. Or most high ratings are given to men and few to women.
- The overall ratings do not agree with the data recorded on the appraisal document.
- The employee is not told how he or she is doing or how this performance bears on the increase.

To avoid these problems, many companies supplement the printed forms and instructions given to supervisors by conducting periodic seminars in the appraisal process. These group sessions stress several key points.

1. *Objectivity*—emphasis on impartiality. Supervisors should avoid basing ratings on personal likes and dislikes or on the employee's appearance, social grace, agreeability, extraversion, or demeanor—unless these are job-related requirements.

2. *Comprehensiveness*—emphasis on all aspects of the job. For example, a sales rep's rating might be based not only on volume of sales but also on success in introducing new products, opening new accounts, training other salespeople, and staying within budget.

3. *Overall qualification*—recognition of the effect of the rating on the employee's status in the range. Does the rating reflect a one-event success or does it represent movement to proper range position based on overall ability?

4. *Dispersion*—holding to a norm. Even when a bell curve is not enforced, supervisors should reasonably expect that "average" ratings do indeed turn out to be the average, with a smaller number of overs and unders.

5. *Communication*—handling the appraisal interview itself. Most supervisors need to develop or refresh their interviewing skills. How to introduce the appraisal, how to make

it productive, how to avoid smoothing-over, how to handle emotions, even how to deal with differing personalities—all these should be reviewed.

PROBLEMS AND RISKS

Nearly everyone would agree that some form of appraisal is desirable. The benefits are obvious. At the same time, no appraisal method seems entirely satisfactory. A number of problems and risks can occur.

Subjectivity. The appraisal reflects the opinions, expectations, and viewpoints of the appraiser just as much as it does the actual performance of the employee. Hence its validity is open to question.

Inconsistency. Supervisor Schmidt, let us say, states job objectives fully and provides clear instructions on how to meet them. In this environment, one employee, Jones, does exceptionally well and receives a high rating. Schmidt's successor, however, leaves it up to employees to figure out what to do and how to do it. In this murky environment Jones now seems unproductive and gets a low rating. Same employee, two different ratings. Which is right? Both? Neither? Of what value are the appraisals that go on record?

Irrelevance. Suppose you are appraising a research nutritionist. The characteristics that your appraisal form tells you to consider—dependability, emotional stability, ability to work with others, effort, productivity, communication, and organizing ability—seem to have little bearing on the fact that this person has done some great work on enzymes. Or you are appraising a supervisor with the "critical incident" system and find no incidents to report. Yet somehow that supervisor seems to run her department so smoothly and unobtrusively that nothing ever goes wrong. But how does this fit into the critical incident assessment?

Unreality. You are asked to tailor your appraisals to a bell curve distribution. You have only four employees reporting to you—although 300 report down the line to them. How do you fit four people into a bell curve, especially if they are about equally proficient? Whether human characteristics naturally fall into a bell curve is in fact debatable. According to D. D. Dorfman, a professor of psychology at the University of Iowa, the normal curve is *not* the rule in nature.* Perhaps a bell curve is simply not appropriate for the group of people you are appraising.

The converse of forcing people into a bell curve is having no dispersion at all. If you rate twenty of your employees as "superior" and one as "average," you may have an elevated perception of what normal is. What does average *mean?* Or, in a different rating system, suppose you rate twenty employees at "far exceeds" and one at "meets requirements." Your superior could easily infer that your requirements are on the low side. Everyone can go beyond them. On the other hand, if all your employees are just satisfactory—if none ever exceeds the level of "average," "competent," "acceptable," or "meets requirements"—it doesn't look as though you have a very lively organization. No fast-track people. No one developing.

None of these conditions is impossible. They do, however, raise questions. And they can create problems, such as:

- Excessive turnover.
- Abnormally high or low comparatio.
- Unfavorable comparisons among parts of the company.

---

* D. D. Dorfman, *Science,* Vol. 201, No. 4362 (1978), p. 1177.

- Failure to adhere to uniform policy.
- Difficulty of managing people who are either underpaid against policy or conscious of a supervisor's desire to appease them with excessive pay increases.

Bias. Your company has an old-time supervisor who believes that virtue consists of coming to work an hour early, staying an hour late, and never complaining. Reporting to him is an employee who gets all her work done well and on time but frequently arrives late and leaves early. Another employee never makes a mistake or misses a deadline but is a habitual complainer and troublemaker. ("These systems are out of date." . . . "We ought to put this in the computer, not do it by hand." . . . "Does anyone ever even look at this report?") What kind of rating will the supervisor give these employees? Are you getting an appraisal of their performance or of the supervisor's hangups?

Noncommunication. "No need to have a formal appraisal review. Employees know in our day-to-day relations how well they're doing." So says a supervisor who hates the embarrassment of a face-to-face discussion of personal progress. He or she especially hates it if certain deficiencies ought to be mentioned. The employee might resent criticism, might be demotivated, might even put up an argument. This supervisor fills out the appraisals at the kitchen table and slips them into the company mail without discussing them at all. How good are appraisals from a supervisor who cannot bear to talk to employees about their performance? "I've worked here for twelve years and in all that time no one has told me how I'm doing," says one of the employees.

EEO Risks. Appraisals not based on objective, verifiable data relating to actual performance are always open to charges of discrimination. This is especially true if "promotability" is an element in the formal appraisal write-up. The appraisal may then be seen as an "employment selection procedure" and may be interpreted as being unfavorable to employees in a class protected by the law.

Unintentional Disclosure. When appraisals have not been fully and honestly communicated to employees, their existence in the files can be dynamite if they subsequently become known. Disclosure may occur, for example, through a court order in an unrelated lawsuit, through simple rummaging in unlocked drawers, or as a result of a new law requiring disclosure of personnel records. Nothing can ignite outrage more than the discovery of a past appraisal, both adverse and unknown.

Some of these problems are inherent in appraisal systems. Others occur when supervisors have not been trained in the appraisal process itself. Because of these problems, appraisal is a field that has received and continues to require much study. We have briefly glanced at it here because it is an important element in salary administration.

9: SALARY INCREASES

SALARY INCREASES CAN be a touchy matter. The employer and the employee are apt to look at them from different viewpoints.

For the employer, a salary increase sparks an immediate jump in cost. But it does not necessarily promote a corresponding jump in productivity. If indeed it did, the employer might wonder if the employee had been holding back until "bribed" to do better. As a matter of fact, the situation is usually the other way around: the increase is given to recognize good work to date. It is a way of saying "We want you to stay with this company and help it prosper."

Nevertheless, there is that jump in costs. What does the employer get for it? Nothing that is easy to see. Certainly a merit increase to the company's parts buyer does not guarantee any change in that buyer's performance. "Ah," says the employer, "but by holding out the opportunity for an increase I motivate that buyer to do a better job. And I use the appraisal process to determine if such improvement has in fact occurred. In the long run, merit increases are paid for out of increased productivity."

This would be very nice if it were verifiable. The trouble is that productivity, despite government statistics on the subject, is often difficult to quantify. On the factory assembly line output measures are no great problem. But on a host of indirect jobs—the billing clerk, the research chemist, the receptionist, the accountant, even the controller and the chief engineer—few companies keep productivity records. Who knows whether the clerk's increase was paid for by increased proficiency in checking invoices or by a remote and profitable change in product mix? Relating any employee's merit increase to productivity is difficult. It may even be undesirable. ("I'm typing 50 percent more letters than I used to, so I ought to get a 50 percent increase!")

The most we can say is that with a corps of experienced employees who are constantly learning more about their jobs and their company and trying to improve, the business runs better than otherwise. So in some hard-to-measure way, the costs of increases are returned.

For employees, the salary increase has a more personal significance. They need it to support the expanding demands of career advancement—the cars, houses, vacations, avocations, marriages, and children with which they hope to enrich their lives. It is expected. And it is expected not just for material reasons. As your employees went through school, they were habituated to periodic report cards and an annual move up to the next grade. Periodic recognition has been built into their lives. The "raise" at work is as duly expected as the "promotion" at school.

In a strict quid-pro-quo economy, none of this might make any sense. People hired to do a certain job either do it satisfactorily or do not. If not, they should be doing something else. If they do perform satisfactorily, they should be given adequate compensation—no less because the employees are new, no more just because they have been around a long time. With this interpretation there would be a single salary for every position. But very few companies follow such a practice. They have salary ranges. And salary ranges mean salary increases to move incumbents up through the range.

Perhaps the basic reason for this arrangement is custom. It is the custom that salaried employees get an increase from time to time. It is the custom that newer employees start at less than the standard rate and then move up over the years. Thus in a junior high school one teacher of algebra may be just out of college, while another may have twenty years of experience. No one would be surprised if the more experienced teacher received a higher salary than the beginner. Yet at the end of the term each teacher has turned out classes of children who have learned the requisite amount of algebra. Both have done what is expected of them. Still, the beginning teacher must await a series of increases before reaching the salary of the senior one. So is it with engineers, accountants, clerks, salespeople, and others. A salary increase from time to time is part of the unwritten bargain. (If a union speaks for the employees, increases become part of the written bargain as well.)

Granted that such a custom exists, why should you observe it? Because if you do not, your better employees will probably move to an employer who does. So you follow the custom.

TYPES OF INCREASES

You begin by describing and evaluating or ranking your salaried positions. You then set a policy on the level of pay you wish to maintain in comparison with other employers competing for people. You conduct surveys and discover the average rates of salary for key benchmark positions, from which you derive those for other jobs in your lineup. From all this you establish a range of salaries for each position, from a minimum to a maximum. You then institute a system for appraising each employee's performance, so that you have a clue to how well that employee is meeting the supervisor's and the job's requirements.

And now, you must assemble all this in a way that permits

you to give periodic salary increases, within the constraints of the system, that are fair and equitable to both you and your employees. Let us consider the various kinds of salary increases you might give.

Salary increases may be classified into several types:

Salary curve adjustment increase
Merit increase
Tenure increase
Progression increase
Promotional increase
Transfer (locality) increase
Reevaluation increase
Temporary increase
Negative increase, or decrease

SALARY CURVE ADJUSTMENT INCREASES

Nature

Various names are given to the salary curve adjustment increase: cost-of-living, inflationary, competitive, market adjustment, level adjustment, range adjustment, economic adjustment. Cost-of-living increase pretty much says what everybody has in mind when they refer to this salary modification. However, "cost of living" is probably a good term to avoid.

The problem with "cost of living" is that your employees may attach different meanings to it. You are altering your salary curve annually to compensate for changes in the going salaries for identifiable jobs. Your employees, however, see cost-of-living statistics almost daily in the newspapers or on television. These vary from month to month. Say you have moved your ranges up 6 percent from last year—fair enough on a twelve-month basis. But today the anchorman on the newscast says, "The Department of Labor has announced that prices have gone up in the last month at an annualized rate of 8.2 percent." "Huh!" says the employee. "The company's holding back on us."

Not only that, so-called cost-of-living indexes vary. They are compiled for various income groups, none of which may match your employees' status. They are weighted for various types of living expense that may or may not reflect those of your employees.

Most important, the term "cost of living" implies that you are paying your employees, not in a competitive marketplace, but according to their needs. Though it may seem brutal to say so, this is exactly what you are *not* doing. Otherwise, your inventory clerk, whose household includes five children, no husband, a senile grandmother, and an arthritic aunt, would get a higher salary than your treasurer, who can live very comfortably on the income from his deceased father's real estate investments. The truth is, if you do adjust your salary curve (and its ranges), you do so only to maintain parity (or a little more or less, according to your policy) with the going rates in the marketplace in which you compete for employees.

In this book we will refer to curve adjustment or range adjustment increases, not cost-of-living increases.

Timing

Some employers, when they adjust the salary curve upward, give everyone a "general increase" at the same time. Others prefer to carry this adjustment into individual salaries throughout the year. In the latter case, the adjustment increase is usually added to the merit increase. Then the employee gets a relatively large salary jump on his or her review date.

The advantages of giving a single, one-time general increase are:

1. It is a clear, public, and unmistakable communication to all employees that the company is staying abreast of salary trends.

2. A general increase now with a merit increase later has a double-whammy effect. It generates two separate periods of good feeling for employees. These morale effects are not to be ignored.

3. Separating the general increase from the merit increase accentuates the dependence of the latter on personal performance. If a merit increase program does have motivational effect, the effect will be most pronounced when the merit increase stands alone.

4. If a group of unionized (hourly or salaried) employees receive periodic increases under a contract, a simultaneous general increase for nonunion salaried employees preserves the necessary relationships. Ratcheting up the nonunion payroll at the same time as the union payroll immediately eliminates compression problems.

5. From a costing point of view a one-time general increase creates an easily identified, readily calculated variance.

Despite these benefits, some employers do not give an across-the-board general increase because of what they see as practical problems:

1. There is an immediate and substantial jump in costs, rather than an upward progression of costs throughout the year. The same is true of demand on working capital.

2. A mass salary increase, all on the same day, creates a community of interest, a topic of discussion, and an opportunity for unfavorable comparisons with the external economy or other employers. All these could be the first steps toward

organizing. No matter what *you* call the increase, employees will call it a cost-of-living increase. They may begin to say, "We"—note the collective "we"—"got only 6 percent, and here's an article in the paper that says prices have gone up 8 percent, and over at such-and-such a company they got 9 percent, and our annual report says profits went up 10 percent." If you start people saying things like this, what have you done?

3. If the general increase is, say, 8 percent, and the merit increase averages around 3 percent, the merit increase looks a little puny. Suppose that everyone received a general range adjustment increase of 8 percent. Ten months later you call Smith into your office and say, "Because you are showing satisfactory progress, as we discussed in our personal performance appraisal session, I am arranging for you to be given a merit increase of 3 percent in your salary. Congratulations!" "Big deal," says Smith to himself. Merit just doesn't seem to be worth much. It has been devalued. Eleven percent would have sounded much better.

4. Individual increases can, when cash is short, be stretched out a month or two. But once a pattern of general increases is established, you are practically committed to it. The increases are then harder to fit to the company's financial circumstances. You have lost your flexibility in running the business.

Sound though these arguments may be, they do have a faint tinge of paranoia. Some companies seem to be able to give one-time general increases and prosper. Others avoid increasing the payroll in one giant step—and they do well, too. The great "if" in the discussion is inflation. When it accelerates too rapidly—and that is exactly what has happened in the United States—general increases are hard to avoid, especially if everyone else is giving them.

MERIT INCREASE

Nature

As mentioned earlier, the primary effect of a merit increase is to move the recipient higher in the salary range for the position filled. The percentage amount of the increase may depend on any of several factors:

1. *Performance appraisal.* This is fairly obvious: the better the performance, the higher the percentage.

2. *Position in range.* Some employers feel that an employee's salary should "grow" fairly rapidly as it moves toward the midpoint. If midpoint is construed as average pay for the average employee everywhere in that type of work, then beyond the midpoint percentage increases should be lower—in other words, salary should grow more slowly. This is a nicety that must be clearly explained to employees. Otherwise, they may wonder why, having demonstrated full proficiency, they don't get the increases they used to.

Employees who for one reason or another are below the range minimum may be given souped-up increases to bring them to minimum in a predetermined period. Conversely, the percentage increase for employees near the maximum may be little or nothing (with the exception of special circumstances mentioned in Chapter 5).

3. *Time since hire or last increase.* Often a new employee is given a small merit increase after the first six months. In fact, some new employees expect it. For this reason, the subject should be covered in the employment interview to prevent misunderstandings. It may be company practice to grant small but frequent increases on lower-level jobs and larger but less frequent increases on higher-level jobs.

4. *Amount of last increase.* This may seem irrelevant, but it can enter the picture. "How can you give Jones a smaller

increase (or a smaller percentage) than last time?" asks Jones's supervisor. "It's demotivating. It's an insult." Not a reasonable argument, perhaps, but it occurs.

Timing

The timing of merit increases also varies among employers. Some of the alternatives are:

1. Give merit increases to all eligible employees at the same time. This practice has the same pros and cons as granting an across-the-board general increase. The alternative is to scatter merit increases throughout the year, which again can be done in various ways.

2. Tie the merit increase in with the timing of the performance appraisal, as described in Chapter 8. This, too, offers opportunity for variation. How often?

3. Grant the merit increase on the anniversary of hire or the anniversary of going on the present job. Either of these simplifies salary administration. It also facilitates personal financial planning by employees.

4. Make the period between increases, as well as the amount of the increase, dependent on performance. Thus an average performer might get a 5 percent merit increase after twelve months while a star performer might get 8 percent after nine months.

5. Modulate the frequency of merit increases to suit the company's financial position. Thus, if profits or cash flow is in a bind, the increase interval could be stretched by a month or two. This is not an uncommon practice and one to which union organizers have a ready answer: "If you can't manage your business right, let the stockholders suffer; don't try to take it out on your employees!" Nevertheless, there are times when keeping the company in good financial condition is in the employees' best interest.

Payment

Merit increases can be paid in either of two ways. In one, the merit increase is treated as an addition to the regular check. For example:

Present salary	$1,000 per month
Increase	5%, or $50 per month
New salary	$1,050 per month

An alternative arrangement is for the employee to continue for six months at the present $1,000 salary and also to receive immediately six months' worth of pay increase ($300) in a lump sum. At the end of six months the ongoing salary is paid at the new level of $1,050. The lump-sum advance can, of course, be for any number of months within the normal review period. Suitable written safeguards should be provided to ensure recapture of the advance if the employee leaves before the period is up.

For the employee, this arrangement provides what amounts to a small interest-free loan to be used for special purposes. It also, at some cost to the company's funds, enhances the perceived significance of the increase.

Accumulated Merit

Some companies give employees an "accumulated merit" increase upon transfer or promotion. For example, Smith is moved into a new position. The move occurs eight months after Smith's last annual performance appraisal and merit increase. At the time of the move, Smith's former supervisor conducts an appraisal and determines that Smith's performance rates a "superior" merit increase of 7 percent. Smith, at the time of the move, is therefore given an immediate increase of $8/12 \times 7\% = 4.67\%$.

An accumulated merit increase is usually given in addition to any promotional increase allowable. There are several advantages to this practice.

1. The appraisal is based on performance in the period to which it applies. Conceivably, performance on the new job, for which the employee is inexperienced, will be misleadingly low.

2. The new supervisor, less familiar with the employee, may not be able to appraise performance on the previous job.

3. The employee starts the new job with a clean slate, knowing that future merit increases depend only on performance on that new job.

4. The employee receives, as part of the transfer or promotion, an additional bump in pay. When a promotional increase is not justified, this addition, which usually comes before the normal review time, is not unwelcome.

TENURE INCREASE

A tenure increase is one that is earned by merely remaining with the employer. Its basic assumptions are that:

- The employee, by not having been fired, is demonstrably doing satisfactory work.
- Experienced employees wise in the company's ways do their work more expeditiously, commit fewer errors, and are more helpful to their colleagues than a constantly changing battery of newcomers.
- The company should encourage loyalty and career service by rewarding the passage of time in its employ.

In large organizations having defined positions and stipulated salary ranges, such a program is about the same as the customary merit increase based on satisfactory performance; and the tenure increases come to a halt when the employee reaches standard (or, alternatively, maximum) salary. In small organizations where people shift about on jobs, fill in for one another, and are not bothered with job titles, tenure increases provide a fair but systematic way of recognizing increasing value to the employer.

PROGRESSION INCREASE

In certain professional or semiprofessional jobs the incumbent progresses from an entry position to a top level. Usually successive stages of progress are identifed in the terminology of the job title. For example: junior engineer, intermediate engineer, senior engineer; assistant product manager, associate product manager, product manager, group product manager; programmer D, C, B, A. Movement from one level to another may be accompanied by a salary increase, and eligibility may depend on:

- The passage of a specified period of time in the lower level—as with a tenure increase.
- The demonstration of personal ability—as with a merit increase.
- The type of work handled—as with a promotional increase. Thus a programmer D may do only elementary jobs in Basic, while a programmer A may program complex systems in Fortran IV or assembler language.
- The amount of supervision required. For example, a junior engineer may work on limited projects under close direction, while a senior engineer may be fully responsible for design, directing several lesser engineers and draftspeople.

Progressive positions are widely extant. They make sense. At the same time, they are difficult to administer. How do you determine when someone is eligible to step up? If tenure is the only qualification, no problem—except that some of your more lackluster employees will move up right along with the winners. Personal ability, reflected in job performance and assayed through performance appraisals, is probably a better guide—subject only to the defects of appraisal systems themselves.

Advancement based on type of work handled or amount of supervision required seems almost foolproof. As in the examples of the programmers and the engineers above, you have merely to define the kinds of tasks required at each level. Then as individuals show that they can do the work, you assign the duties to them and pay accordingly. The trouble is that the work at hand doesn't always sort itself out so neatly. You get rushed and have to assign an intermediate engineer to a troubleshooting job normally done by a senior. Or a programmer D says, "Hey, I can do Fortran. How about putting me on some heavier assignments?" Unfortunately, you don't have any at the moment. Pretty soon the work or the ability of people to do it doesn't bear much relationship to the job title—or the pay level. Thus, though the progressive levels can be defined neatly on paper, it is difficult to hold the work assignments in place in practice.

Some companies attempt to get around these problems by setting quotas: "About 20 percent of the work is top level, about 30 percent is next, and 35 percent more is below that; the remaining 15 percent of the staff should be at entry level. So we'll set quotas for four programmers at the A level, six at B, seven at C, and three at D." After a while, a programmer C shows up in the personnel office and says, "I'm doing exactly the same work as Smith, who is a B. How come I'm not a B?" Now all you have to do is tell him why: the quota for Bs is full. Good luck.

Again, progression systems make sense, but they are difficult to administer. Because of pressure from employees, they tend to get overloaded in the upper brackets.

PROMOTIONAL INCREASE
What Is a Promotion?

An employee gets promoted to a better job, so he or she gets an increase in pay. Fair enough. Now, then: Just what constitutes a promotion? And how much increase should go with it? First, let's clarify what we mean by promotion. If an employee is moved to another job in the same grade, that is a *transfer*, not a promotion.

But say that the employee, Jones, is moved to a job in a slightly higher grade and has to train for six months in order to learn it. During that period the boss or the previous incumbent or other employees have to help out. In a sense Jones has been promoted, perhaps even has the job title, and is seen by the world as filling the job. Yet Jones is not really *doing* the job. If Jones is to get a promotional increase—when?

Take another case. Johns, a developmental engineer, has been installing a new process in Department A. Now it is decided to appoint Johns supervisor of Department A. Johns will get experience in handling people and meeting production goals and thus have a broader base for future advancement. But both jobs carry the same salary range. In a way it looks as though Johns has been promoted, yet on the books there is no change.

Another case. You don't have salary grades. Rather, you have a separate salary range for each job. Schmidt is moved from a job with a standard (or midpoint) salary of $1,000 to one with a standard salary of $1,030. Schmidt is progressing upward, it is true, but a change of only 3 percent seems too small to be called a promotion. Now suppose that Schmidt is pretty good and the company is growing and Schmidt earns a number of these small upward boosts. After a while, Schmidt is on a job with a standard salary of $1,100. Even if no one step seemed like a promotion, overall something very like a promotion has occurred.

Now consider George, an hourly paid stockroom attendant. You decide to move George to a salaried job as stock records clerk in the office. The take-home pay is no better, but the working conditions and opportunity for advancement are. "Wow!" says George. "Promoted at last! Do I get an increase?"

And here is Novak, a long-term employee who has risen to the max of the job filled. Now Novak is appointed group leader. A comparison of the two jobs is shown in Figure 24. Novak is already making more than the midpoint of the new job. A promotional increase would take Novak so close to the max of the new job, on which Novak is relatively inexperienced, that there would be little room for further growth.

Then there's Lyle, a messenger who has just earned a marketing degree in night school and can now fill an opening as product assistant. How the two jobs compare is illustrated in Figure 25. There is an 80 percent differential between Lyle's present salary and the minimum of the new job. Should Lyle be given a gigantic 80 percent promotional increase? You could probably keep Lyle happy with 30 percent. On the other hand, is it fair to pay less to Lyle, a loyal employee, than to a stranger you would, so to speak, hire from the street?

And now Pelli, a supervisor of a department carrying a standard salary of $2,000. Pelli has been made manager of a group of departments, a position with a standard salary of $3,000. Clearly, here is a promotion! But what about all those others?

Figure 24. Novak's promotion.

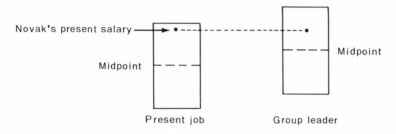

Figure 25. Lyle's promotion.

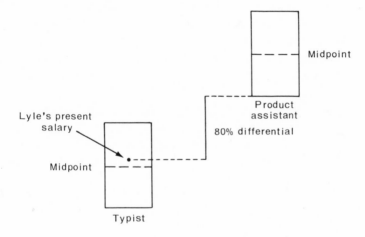

Working Rules

In looking at these examples, we can see that what constitutes a promotion is a cloudy matter. On the one hand, if you dole out a "promotional increase" with every job change, sooner or later you will have some people who are overpaid in comparison with those who combine experience with stability. On the other hand, if you suit the increase to the person, giving some people a promotional increase and others none according to what you can get away with, you're heading for trouble.

Accordingly, many companies find it helpful to develop a set of working rules to cover promotional increases. The exact specifications vary from company to company, depending on internal custom, job relationships, and pay scales, but they often include the following:

1. Any person permanently transferred or promoted to another position shall receive at least the minimum of the salary range for that position.

2. A promotion is defined as a transfer from position A to position B such that the salary midpoint of B is at least X percent above that of A.

3. An employee receiving a promotion shall also receive a promotional increase of Y percent in salary in addition to accumulated merit increase.

4. Employees fully qualified for the position promoted to shall receive the promotional increase effective as of the date to which they move to that position. For others, the promotional increase shall be effective upon completion of a probationary period not to exceed Z months.

5. Salary, including merit and promotional increases, shall not exceed the maximum of the range of the position promoted to.

6. Employees transferred from hourly to salary payroll shall be eligible for a promotional increase only if they meet the requirements of rule 2, except that the individual's average straight-time hourly earnings of the job promoted from shall be used instead of salary midpoint.

7. Any employee receiving a series of transfers, none of which separately qualifies for a promotional increase, shall

receive a promotional increase when the accumulated change in the midpoints of successive jobs amounts to X percent.

Rules of this sort rest on an assumption: that a promotion should be accompanied by a monetary reward. However, it can also be said that there is sufficient reward in the prestige, career advancement, and higher available salary range. With this thinking no promotional increase would be granted except one necessary to move the employee to, or nearer to, the minimum of the new job.

This is a fairly hardnosed, save-the-money approach. Granting promotional increases is probably more in line with employee expectations. In the long run it may contribute to performance improvement by fostering feelings of success, rather than deprivation, among upwardly mobile people— those who can improve your business.

TRANSFER (LOCALITY) INCREASE

Companies operating in several locations may have different salary scales for different parts of the country. These are intended to recognize variations in the cost of living between, say, New York City and a small town in Texas.

With such an arrangement, an employee moved to a high-cost area receives, in addition to any other increases, an increment to cover the locality change. This increment is part of ongoing salary, not to be compared with a one-time relocation allowance for the physical move itself.

This seems very reasonable, in fact essential. You move a salesperson from Wachiroo to New York, and at the same time you move her to the New York salary curve. But what happens when you move her from New York to Wachiroo? Do you *cut* her pay correspondingly? What do you say? "Look, you've done such a swell job in the Big Apple that we're going to put you where they're really crying for your talent—down there in beautiful Wachiroo, where you won't need a winter coat. You'll get an accumulated merit increase of 6 percent and a locality adjustment of minus 10 percent. But believe me, you'll come out way ahead! *Way* ahead!"

To get around this difficulty some companies pay a locality differential in a separate check so that the recipient will remember what it's for.

Of course, one way out is just to forget about the differential when making a downhill transfer. Let it ride as a sort of hidden increase. This opens the door to two other problems. First, your transferee is now out of line with other employees in the new locality. Second, you'll have to figure out what to do if your salesperson gets transferred again—say, to San Francisco. Do you give a *second* locality increase? Maybe the separate check idea isn't so bad.

REEVALUATION INCREASE

From time to time, an existing position gets reevaluated and moved into a higher salary range. This may occur (1) because the original evaluation was wrong or (2) because additional requirements have been laid on the job that do in fact upgrade it.

The second case is equivalent to the creation of a new job. To give an increase, if justified under your promotional rules, is a fair response to such a change. Sticking to some sort of rule is, however, important. Otherwise you will be asked for an increase every time a few duties are added to a job. What counts is whether the duties changed the job sufficiently to raise its ranking—and, if so, whether they raised it enough to provide an increase under your guidelines. Look at it the other way around: When a job is simplified slightly, do you cut the incumbent's salary?

The first case is a little different. Nothing that the job incumbents are doing has changed. Only the evaluation is different. You can deal with this in several ways. One is to provide any increase necessary to bring the incumbents at least to the new minimum. A second approach goes a little further: increasing the incumbents' pay in such a way as to maintain position in the range—in other words, placing them at the same percentage of midpoint in the new range that they occupied in the old one. A third approach is to give them retroactive pay for the period in which the job was underevaluated. (This introduces a further complication: What do you do about people who moved in and out of the job in the interim?) A fourth is to do nothing.

Reevaluations present a problem. Once they are recognized as a source of increases, pressure arises to have many jobs reevaluated—always upward. The requests for downward reevaluations will be few. Moreover, since debatable evaluations always exist, the most aggressive and articulate people will be the ones most likely to obtain revisions. Sections of the organization will then experience a slight upsurge in their salary level, which will be reflected in the firm's overall cost of doing business.

It is a good rule to consider each evaluation as locked in unless there is a significant change in requirements. Should a time come when complaints of misevaluation are really clamorous, an overall review should be made of all jobs. This will correct the overevaluations as well as the underevaluations.

TEMPORARY INCREASE

Now and then an employee is away from the job for an extended period because of maternity, illness, special assignment, vacation, education, or family emergency. Then a lower-level employee fills in until the absentee returns. Should this employee be given any special salary consideration?

Some companies say no. The fill-in employee is in all likelihood not performing all the duties of the one replaced, not performing them as well, and in need of greater supervision. Moreover, the temporary advancement is valuable preparation for the future.

Other companies favor a temporary increase to the fill-in employee. This can be made contingent on some stipulated time period—say, at least one month in the replacement job. At the end of the replacement period the temporary increase expires and the employee returns to the former salary (plus, of course, any interim merit increases that may have accrued). The amount of the increase may be the difference between the employee's salary and the range minimum of the replacement job or X percent, whichever is greater.

Although the temporary increase adds slightly to costs, you can make a good case for it. It is fair to the employee, especially if he or she is keeping the old job going while handling added duties. It stifles any possible feelings that the company is getting something for nothing. And, if the fill-in job is a supervisory one, it enhances the employee's sense of self-worth—essential in exercising authority.

NEGATIVE INCREASE (DECREASE)

Salary administrators must occasionally cope with the unpleasant question of whether an employee should receive a decrease in salary.

Ordinarily a decrease comes only with a demotion. But every demotion does not call for a decrease. For example, you certainly wouldn't cut the pay of an employee whom you moved to a lower job in order to straighten out an operational or organizational mess for which high-level talents were temporarily needed. Or one who was being placed in a lower-paying job as part of a learning and career-broadening program. Or one who temporarily filled a vacant lower position until a new incumbent could be recruited.

At the same time, there are some demotional moves that might or might not justify reduction in salary. For example:

1. Mental, emotional, or physical problems prevent employee from continuing on present job.
2. Employee cannot meet goals on present job, though the record shows he or she could do so on previous job, to which a return demotion can be made.
3. Reorganization or cutback in the workforce eliminates present job. Employee can bump downward to a lower job.
4. Change in operating procedures guts present job, so that it evaluates at a markedly lower level.
5. Change in operating systems or procedures eliminates present job.
6. Change in organization structure moves position down in the hierarchy so that, with less freedom and authority, it evaluates lower.
7. New supervisor finds employee persona non grata and demands expulsion from present position.
8. Employee is removed from job in order to make it available as career step for a more promising employee.
9. Job was incorrectly evaluated too high to begin with.

These reasons present a mixed bag. Some are attributable to the employee's failings. Some are for the employer's convenience. Some arise from the inevitable changes that occur in the progress of a business. You can handle them in any of several ways.

1. Set a hard-and-fast rule. *Every* demotion is accompa-

nied by an immediate reduction in salary—say, to at most the maximum of the new job. Reasons:

- Uniform, impersonal treatment.
- Avoidance of the spectacle of high-paid employees on low-salaried jobs, which may seem unfair to others
- Avoidance of unfavorable cost of overpaid employees.

2. Same as method 1 except that the salary reduction is carried out in stages over a period of time. Reasons:

- The employee, relying on an unwritten contract from the employer, has incurred financial commitments from which it will take time to get free.
- The employee's salary rose gradually over time, and there were periods when it was well below the average, or midpoint. It is only fair that it should decline in the same way.

3. Reduce salary by method 1 or 2 only when demotion is "employee's fault."

4. Make no reduction in salary. Carry the employee at a red-circle salary on lower job, with no increase until the salary range rises high enough to encompass red-circle salary. Reasons:

- Reduces likelihood of having a demotivated, demoralized, disgruntled employee.
- Sustains, among other employees, image of company as a compassionate, secure employer.

It may be argued that anyone should rejoice at being able to keep a job at all, even with reduced play. In Maurice Chevalier's famous phrase (when asked how it felt to be an old man), "Consider the alternative." But most people don't think that way.

Whether you have the problem of negative pay increases depends on a more basic question: whether you permit demotions to occur. Some employers prefer separation to demotion. If you do demote, you should have an established rule to go by.

PROBLEMS AND RISKS

From the employee's point of view, a salary increase can never entail a risk, and it poses a problem only if it is too small. Many supervisors, too, favor liberal increases. It is easy to be generous with somebody else's money. Only a tight-fisted curmudgeon could see actions that secure the blessings of prosperity to the company's employees as anything but wholly desirable. Yet somewhere in the area of salary increases lie the seeds of future difficulties if control is not exercised.

Lack of Guidelines. Salary increases, properly administered, do a lot to retain desirable employees and bind them to the company. On a subject as tricky as this, properly means fairly. And fairly means fairly in the eyes of the employees.

Often employees discuss their salaries more openly than management might wish. (In fact, they sometimes exaggerate salaries as a matter of one-upmanship.) If your salary administration smacks of caprice, they'll be unhappy. Only written guidelines, consistently adhered to, can ensure fair treatment to all. The guidelines may or may not be made public, but if it is known that they exist, allegations of inequitable salary administration will be minimized.

Lack of Mobility. In a relatively static organization, few promotions occur. As a result, employees tend to remain for long periods of time in the same position. They then float up to the top of the salary ranges, and further increases, if given beyond the max, tend to elevate company payroll costs compared with those of competitors. This can become a problem of costs versus morale. Perhaps the firm should be prepared to lose a few employees who, having reached max, can increase their earnings only by finding another job. A natural exodus may be preferable to the inevitable forced one caused by insupportable budgets.

Salary Squeezing. Stretching out or minimizing salary increases in order to brighten the profit picture may not be good business. It distresses and alienates the very people on whom you rely for profit improvement. ("They have to pay the going rate for electricity and raw materials. Why not for bookkeepers and technicians?" "So they didn't know how to run the business for a profit. Why put the bite on us?") Perhaps your economies should come, not from salary squeezing but from workforce reduction. Better a house full of well-paid servants than a palace full of grumblers.

Issue Confusion. Periodic marketplace adjustments in the salary ranges can make it appear as though the company is keeping up with the times. But they are meaningless unless they are followed up—either at once or throughout the year—with corresponding increases in actual salaries. (Confusion over actual salaries and official salary ranges was at the heart of the scenarios in Chapter 7.) Furthermore, even increases in actual salaries will not advance employees in the ranges without supplementary merit, progression, or tenure increases. Thus disguising as a merit increase the range adjustment given to the nurse you hired last year keeps her at the same level as this year's graduates. Compression has set in.

Sometimes a management that does not understand the

distinctions among curve adjustment, salary adjustment, and the other forms of increase gets a confused picture. The risk is that salaries will get out of line—either too high or too low—without management's knowing what is happening.

Overgenerosity. As mentioned before, many supervisors tend to be generous, both with appraisals and with increases. ("Makes for a happy, productive workforce. Pays off in the long run.") Maybe. But if you are making valid surveys, have set your salary curve to be competitive with other employers, and have developed realistic guidelines to support your policy, a preponderance of very large increases is going to give you a high comparatio and a higher-than-planned cost level. Controls are needed to counter the risk of unplanned payroll escalation.

Intracompany Variability. A common problem is overgenerosity in some areas of the company accompanied by undergenerosity in others. "I give all my nonexempts minimum increases," boasts a sales manager. "They're easily replaced. That leaves more money to hand out to my salespeople." Or: "I hold back on increases to my supervisors," says the manager of Factory A. "Where else could they find a job if they didn't like it here?" But: "I go overboard on increases to my supervisors," says the manager of Factory B. "I mean, they're right at the cutting edge where we make or lose money. I want them to feel good." It is difficult to argue that these various philosophies don't *work*. They probably do. But you'll have problems, all the same, especially when you try to transfer an employee from a rich climate to a stingy one, or when employees in these two climates compare notes.

Poor Communication. Relying on salary action to carry its own message is a form of noncommunication. Thus a supervisor says, "Pat is not doing good work. Maybe if we hold back on his increase, it will shock him into doing better." And maybe not. Pat may in fact feel that:

"The boss has a grudge against me."

"The boss has forgotten about me."

"They're having financial problems."

"Okay, no increase, no effort."

Poor performance should be addressed directly. The supervisor should find what causes it and work out corrective action. Secret signals via the salary increase system are apt to be ineffective.

Premature Promises. "Hope deferred," says the proverb, "maketh the heart sick." Promising increases in advance is a good way to raise hope. Some companies regard it as a form of motivation. "You just learn all the ins and outs of this job and turn in a good performance, and I'll see that you get a 10 percent salary increase next September." To the employee, this sounds like a guaranteed increase. Then September rolls around and there are budget problems or perhaps the employee hasn't looked all *that* good, and the 10 percent isn't forthcoming. Now we have a demotivated employee. As a matter of fact, an employee who thinks the increase is in the bag probably wasn't given much motivation to start with. A promise to have a performance appraisal at the appropriate time and to follow the guidelines is probably all that is necessary.

Rigidity. Rules and guidelines are great, and you should have them. But they are intended to benefit the company, not cripple it. You'll want to be careful that the house bureaucrat isn't administering your salary system to the company's detriment. For example:

Supervisor Says:	*Bureaucrat Replies:*
My top researcher, a national authority in his field who is working on a key project, is at the top of his range. Can't I give him a raise anyway?	Nope. Would take him over max. Besides, he'd soon be making as much as his boss.
Smith has been falling behind in her work. I'd like to hold back on a raise pending better performance.	If Smith doesn't qualify for a minimum increase, she should be fired. Company policy doesn't allow deferring increases.
There's a big demand for swivel engineers. Unless we give our three engineers maximum increases to meet competitive rates, we'll lose them.	Impossible. You have to stick with the bell curve. One can get a "max" increase, one a "superior," and one a "meets expectations."
For some reason we seem to be paying the highest rate in town for switchboard operators. Let's hold back on increases until they fall in line.	Can't do it. The rules call for a range adjustment plus a merit increase, and we have to stick to the rules.
We're going to have to move Jones, the president's secretary, to a clerical job on account of her arthritis. She's getting on in years. But we'd like not to cut her salary.	Out of the question! People get paid for the jobs they are doing. She's being demoted, so she gets a reduction in pay.

Each of these cases is being handled correctly, you might say, by the salary administrator. At the same time, each is so special, and (if sensitively dealt with) so unlikely to create a precedent, that it seems to deserve individualized treatment. In the last case—that of an elderly person being demoted—the risks of age discrimination charges cannot be ignored.

10: SALARY BUDGETING

Some parts of your business you can control and some you can't. You would like, of course, to control the financial end results: at the close of the year, more money should have come in than went out. But can you?

The "come in" part—revenue—is not entirely yours to command. Your marketing and sales efforts—these you can manipulate. But the actions of your competitors, the state of the economy, and the technosociological trends that float your business up and down—these things you have to cope with rather than manage. They aren't entirely in your hands.

At first glance it may seem that you have more control over the "went out" part—expenses. You don't have to spend money unless you want to. But here again external forces are at work. The economy, your suppliers, and regulatory agencies are all nibbling on your financial margins. What can you do about them? Not everything you'd like to.

For these reasons it is essential that you keep a firm grip on those elements of the business that you *can* get hold of. One way to do this, of course, is through budgeting. And one of the elements that you can control through budgeting is salary expense.

REASONS FOR SALARY BUDGETING

A salary budget is a forecast, made before the next fiscal year, of the salary expense that will be incurred for that year. With it you can:

1. *Hold salary expense in line.* No changes in salary levels will be permitted unless they have been budgeted.

2. *Ensure equitable treatment to employees.* Provision will be made in advance for range adjustments and merit increases so that these can be handled in as fair and orderly a manner as possible.

3. *Forecast cash flow.* The amount of funds to meet salary payrolls will be established in advance so that cash requirements can be planned for.

4. *Plan business actions.* The need to increase or decrease the salary payroll to reflect business changes will be foreseen and treated as part of the business plan rather than as an emergency.

5. *Determine costs.* Overhead expenses will be allocated to products or services in accordance with budgeted amounts.

If your salary budget is to be of any consequence at all, these are ends well worth pursuing.

BUDGET COMPONENTS

In formulating a salary budget, you may find it helpful to break the budget into two separate components. The first component is the number of people required. How many positions, how many bodies, are needed in each section of the company? The simplest and most obvious approach is to prepare a list of the positions in each department. However, if your objective is to reduce expenses—particularly overhead expenses, which often fall in the fixed category—you can go further than merely listing. As an approach to cost reduction you can *analyze.* How to analyze the need for salary positions is described in the following sections.

The second component of the salary budget is individual salaries. For each position listed, what level of pay will occur throughout the coming year? This, too, can be analyzed separately.

STAFFING PROBLEMS

Constructing a reasonable salary budget is never easy, since you face many conflicting pressures. On the one hand, you have people sincerely interested in improving quality, product design, facilities, safety, employee skills, working conditions, customer service, sales volume, personnel resources, research, maintenance, and all the other things for which they are directly accountable. To meet these objectives, people need an adequate force of employees. On the other hand, you have a financial imperative. Revenues must exceed outlays by X percent. Not three years from now, but in the year for which you are budgeting. A workforce that gets too large now, even if in preparation for a rosy future, chomps into that excess.

The conflict of pressures amounts to this: Should you spend money for the good of the business or should you save money for the good of the business? Whether yours is a small operation or a giant one, a hospital, a college, a foundation, a church, or a professional association, you are caught in the jaws of this vise. Only in mushrooming industries or (to the consumer's eye, at least) in the monopolistic utilitylike companies does there seem to be an absence of budget pressure on salary payroll.

Reducing the salary payroll is never easy. It is an inescapable law of physics that where pressure exists, there is resistance to it. The resistance takes various forms. Thus supervisors may budget for unfilled positions. Indefinite post-ponements in filling them provide a cushion against unto-ward events. Alternatively, requests for budget reduction may be met by virtuous excision of positions never filled, with associated claims of "savings."

There may be a stockpile of trainees and backups to pro-vide for future growth or turnover. There may be sufficient employees to provide for any conceivable spurt in workload or in absenteeism. There may even be plans for adding posi-tions. These are customarily introduced in a confidential talk with the boss, beginning with the familiar disclaimer, "I am in no way interested in empire building, but . . . ." Then fol-lows a reasoned explanation of how three more people are essential to handle increasingly onerous government require-ments, to achieve operating economies, to attain quality con-trol objectives, to sign on new accounts, or to fully realize the potential of the company computer.

All these measures may be perfectly legitimate. But if in the course of salary budgeting the costs seem to be inching up to the high side, that list of budgeted positions deserves a close look. A primary reason is that high salary expense is not necessarily attributable to high salaries. It may be due to too many salaries—which in turn reflect vague assignments, un-necessary work, poor supervision, confused work flow, re-work, and other devourers of salaried man-hours.

STAFFING ANALYSIS

Organizations that are clearly expanding, noncompetitive, and well funded characteristically have more "give" in their payroll than those that are fighting an uphill battle. If you are in the prosperous group, your salary budget may well be based on the existing number of people plus whatever re-cruitment is foreseen for growth.

If, on the other hand, you are engaged in financial mountain climbing, you may wish to discover if an excess of salaried positions is one of the impedimenta holding you back. For every position on the payroll you should then ask: Which does more for the business—spending the money on salary or spending it on advertising to build market share, on new equipment to reduce cost, or possibly on higher inventory levels to improve customer service? Or, in fact, letting a savings on salary drop through to the profit line?

Several techniques for salary force regulation are described below. None of them is supereffective in all circumstances, but they can be of some value.

"Voluntary" Reduction. Supervisors are asked to carefully review staffing and eliminate unnecessary positions. This plea produces mixed results. Some supervisors go along; some dig in their heels. Many get upset and deny that they have superfluous positions.

"Stipulated" Reduction. Supervisors are told that there will be a moratorium on hiring, or an across-the-board reduction of X percent in the number of salaried employees. In certain parts of the enterprise, however, either of these nonselective actions may do more harm than good.

Time-and-Methods Study. On many clerical jobs, time standards can be established for repetitive elements: so many minutes per line entry, so many per 100 lines of typing. With such standards, it is possible to determine staffing for a given volume of clerical work done at reasonable efficiency. With less precision, this approach can be carried to other types of jobs. For example, the average unit call time and travel time of sales representatives and customer service specialists can be approximated as a basis for standards of performance.

From these numbers you can figure how many people you need for a given level of activity.

Peak Employment Elimination. Smoothing the peaks can help reduce salary commitments. Examination of the number of employees available may disclose that you have geared your staffing to periodic spurts—special sales, custom orders, month-end closings, seasonal swings, emergencies, and the like. An alternative is to employ freelancers, consultants, service bureaus, or temporary employees for the crests instead of carrying a permanently swollen payroll. Permanently staff only for the average, not the peak.

Overhead Value Analysis. This is a technique for examining the functions of each position (and the time involved) in order to eliminate the least necessary functions and thereby reduce man-hours. Since the study involves the employees themselves, it can be both effective and disruptive.

Zero-Base Budgeting. This extension of overhead value analysis relies on supervisory ranking of job functions in terms of essentiality or disposability. The idea is to sacrifice the least needed. The merits of this approach are those of cost reduction; the defects, if any, are the large amount of time, paperwork, and review required along with the opportunities for "sandbagging" by judicious ranking of indispensable services last.

Organizational Systems Analysis. If the two previous techniques may be called "micro," since they address individual positions, organizational systems analysis may be termed "macro," since it looks at the organization as a whole. The analysis involves a study of overall organizational objectives and the means employed to attain them. In doing so, it particularly considers the interplay of authority, accountability, and information flow among the parts of the company in order to discover functions that are duplicative, dead-ending, or obsolete as well as functions that are not currently being performed but should be. Because it is organization-oriented, the analysis differs from the more limited systems studies associated with accounting and data processing activities.

None of these techniques for reducing salary costs will make people happy. But if your competitors keep their business going with a lean crew, can you afford to be fat?

SALARY LEVELS

To a certain extent, you can determine unilaterally how many people your budgeted payroll will cover. You have somewhat less freedom in determining the salary levels that those people will receive. This introduces a degree of uncertainty in your forecasting. Several variables can affect salary levels, and hence your budget.

Economic Trends

In your budgeting you must allow for changes in the general competitive market level of salaries. In times of a cheapening dollar this amounts to an inflationary adjustment. But it is not necessarily true that salaries advance at, for instance, the rate of change in the consumer price index issued by the Bureau of Labor Statistics. For example, as shown in Figure 26, salaries for drafters moved faster than the change in the consumer price index for four of the eight years shown. In three of the years the consumer price index rose more than salaries. Only in one year was there parity. The two don't track.

Your problem is to estimate, first, by how much the general salary level will have risen one year hence and, second, how this increase will spread itself over your fiscal year. Moreover, you must separate local and national effects. If you are

Figure 26. Drafters' salaries versus consumer price index.

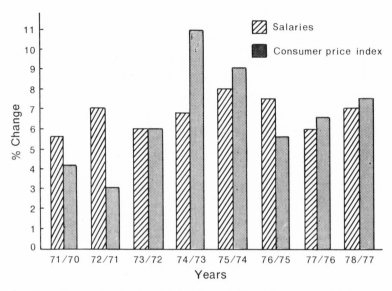

SOURCE: Bureau of Labor Statistics Bulletin 2004 and Department of Labor.

in a depressed, labor-surplus area, your general salary level may rise less on nonexempt employees than on the professionals for whom you compete in a national market.

Merit or Progressive Increases

Your budget must also provide for merit increases. If you have been giving merit or progressive increases to move employees up through the salary ranges, you are probably locked into this practice. It is expected as part of the unwritten understanding between you and your employees. Therefore you have to provide for it in the budget.

At the same time you do have some control over the frequency and amount of these increases. Giving them early and large, with a fair amount of "superior" ratings, will, in Shakespeare's words, bind your employees to you with hoops of steel—at least until the next increase is due. Giving them late and small will cause some dissatisfaction but will probably not lead to a mass exodus. You can get away with scrimping now and then, but once you become identified as a low-pay employer you may experience a change in personnel. At any rate, your task is to forecast any movement in total salaried payroll level due to merit increases. In a subsequent section we will review this task in more detail.

Turnover

If your year were to end just as it began—with the same employees, all on the same jobs—a forecast of market level and merit changes would be all that is needed for budgeting. Another factor enters, however, and this is turnover. Turnover affects the general salary level.

For example, if you have employees who will retire or resign in the coming year, to be replaced by newcomers, this change in mix will slightly lower the general salary level. Low-salary-range incumbents are stepping into the shoes of high-level ones.

If you are contracting or expanding your salaried force, the change may affect the general salary level for which you are budgeting. Who will leave—the youngest employees or those highest in their ranges? Who will come in—novices or thoroughly experienced professionals who will be range-high? If you expect promotions to occur, managerships to be created or eliminated, or internal functions to be turned over to outside contractors, these changes may also affect your salary mix.

Other Variables

The timing of salary-level changes also influences the budget. Is a range adjustment increase given en masse, or is it parceled out over the year? Do merit and tenure increases cluster, because of past practices, in specific months? If they come near the beginning of the year, your total salary budget will of course be higher than if they are spread uniformly over the twelve months.

In addition to all the variables mentioned, special one-time circumstances, usually foreseeable, must be taken into account. Organizational realignments, job reevaluation programs, spinoffs and acquisitions, policy revisions, and make-versus-buy decisions—all these can affect both the size of the salaried force and its salary level. Indirectly, changes in vacation, holidays, time off, and overtime pay provisions may have a bearing.

DETAILED BUDGETING

A not uncommon method of salary budgeting is to prepare a line-by-line, month-by-month forecast for the coming year. An example for a small department is shown in Figure 27. For this example it is assumed that:

1. A general range adjustment increase of 6 percent will be given to all salaried employees in August.

2. The merit increase schedule is:

Outstanding	7%
Superior	5%
Satisfactory	3%

3. Smith, the supervisor, may retire on June 1, to be replaced by Jones, who will receive a 10 percent promotional increase. Smith will receive an earned month's vacation pay in June.

4. Jones will probably receive a 5 percent merit increase in October, if performing as expected as a supervisor.

5. An additional clerk will be hired at the entry level on May 1.

Thus the material needed for preparation of this budget consists of both factual data and estimates. The factual data

Figure 27. Salary budget.

SALARY BUDGET – FISCAL YEAR 19____

Department Name _____ No. _____ Preparation Date _____

Job Title	Job No.	Name	Empl. No.	Jan.	Feb.	Mar.	Apr.	May	Jun.	Jul.	Aug.	Sep.	Oct.	Nov.	Dec.	Total
Supervisor	0963	J. Smith	0122	2,000	2,000	2,000	2,000	2,000	2,000	–	–	–	–	–	–	12,000
Supervisor	0963	L. Jones	0425	–	–	–	–	–	1,320	1,320	1,399	1,399	1,469	1,469	1,469	9,845
Clerk	0889	L. Jones	0425	1,200	1,200	1,200	1,200	1,200	–	–	–	–	–	–	–	6,000
Clerk	0889	D. Myles	0438	1,000	1,000	1,000	1,030	1,030	1,030	1,030	1,092	1,092	1,092	1,092	1,092	12,580
Clerk	0889	S. Hayes	0527	900	900	900	900	900	945	945	1,002	1,002	1,002	1,002	1,002	11,400
Clerk	0889	Vacant		–	–	–	–	800	800	800	848	848	848	848	848	6,640
Typist	0625	W. Smart	0613	650	650	650	650	650	650	650	689	689	710	710	710	8,058
TOTAL				5,750	5,750	5,750	5,780	6,580	6,745	4,745	5,030	5,030	5,121	5,121	5,121	66,523

are the names, positions, and present salaries of the various employees. The estimated data include:

- Best guess as to the amount of general increase that survey data will suggest for the August date.
- Likelihood of Smith's retiring on June 1 and being replaced by Jones.
- Need to hire a new clerk in May to prepare for the vacancy created by Jones's promotion.
- Timing and amount of merit increases for the various employees, based on informal opinion in advance of more exact information at appraisal time.
- January names and salaries, assuming the budget is prepared several months in advance.

Laborious though this compilation may seem, it is fairly easy to perform, especially if each supervisor does it for the employees he or she directs. As a simplifying measure, a "satisfactory" rating may be assumed for all employees. Then an overall percentage can be added to the total to allow for the companywide dispersion of advanced ratings.

Some employers have found it convenient to run precalculated increases through their computer to produce budget schedules. The supervisor can then adjust the schedules for expected separations, transfers, or hires.

It should be understood that the salary budget is not an irrevocable commitment. It is a statement of expectations. How well you can live within it depends on a host of external circumstances, not the least of which is actual performance throughout the year in other, nonsalary segments of the total company budget. Most of all, it should be understood that the salary increases tentatively laid out for budgeting are by no means guarantees.

UNIT BUDGETING

An alternative to working out a line-by-line, name-by-name, job-by-job forecast of next year's payroll is to estimate the total salary cost of the organization taken as a unit. In this method, the "organization" may be either the whole company, if it is quite small, or an individual department. The calculation may be performed in several brief steps:

1. Estimate the total salary expense for the unit for the beginning of the fiscal year.

2. Multiply this number by the estimated percentage of *merit* (or tenure) increases to be granted through the year. For example, suppose that your average merit increase is 5 percent. If the increases are distributed fairly evenly over the year, the effective annual increase is 2.5 percent. This is the figure that you multiply by the starting payroll to arrive at the increment in the estimated new annual payroll. If, however, the increases cluster at the beginning or end of the year, the effective percentage is correspondingly more or less.

3. Multiply the figure obtained above by the estimated percentage of *range adjustment* increases to be incurred in the coming year. Again, consideration must be given to when these increases will occur. If you plan a cloudburst for a single date, the percentage should be adjusted for the number of months they will be effective. If the increases will be spread throughout the year, you should treat them in the same way as merit increases. For example, if you think that the range adjustment increase—the one that brings your employees in line with the external market—will be 6 percent, and if you plan to grant it to all employees at the end of the first quarter, the total year's salary budget will be 4.5 percent (6% × .75) higher than the year-entry level. If, on the other hand, you plan to pepper the payroll with individual range adjustment increases, scattered evenly over the twelve months, the year will average 3 percent (6% × .5) higher than the entry level.

4. Deduct the expected annual cost of net reductions from the personnel roster; or add the expected annual cost of net expansion in the personnel roster. Both these figures, of course, are estimated for the number of months of the year that they will be effective.

If your workforce is relatively young and stable, this estimate should be fairly accurate. However, if you have high turnover, with relatively large numbers of high-in-the-range employees being replaced by entrants, the average salary may shift downward. Conversely, if you are expanding and have to hire highly qualified people from other companies, the average salary will be higher than otherwise. In either of these cases, a correction must be applied to your figures.

Some companies carry the unit budgeting concept forward into the apportioning of increases throughout the year. To do so, they allocate to each supervisor a "pot" of money to be used for increases. How this "pot" is meted out among the employees is left to the supervisor's discretion. With such a program supervisory autonomy and authority are certainly strengthened. And the clerical drudgery of name-by-name budgeting is avoided—no small benefit. Nevertheless, the practice has its drawbacks. For one thing, inequitable treatment may develop among supervisors. Are the employees *company* employees, entitled to equal treatment, or are they each supervisor's employees? For another, not all good supervisors are good financial managers. What happens if some of them use up the "pot" too early in the year? Do the unreached employees go hungry?

Rather than apply percentages to the beginning salary level for the fiscal year, you can apply them to the total salary cost (if you can estimate it) for the preceding year. In this case you will not, of course, have to modify your increase percentages for the number of months that they are effective. But you can use this method only if you expect increases to fall in the same months as in the base year.

STANDARD-COST METHOD

Our discussion so far has assumed that departments are charged with the actual salaries incurred. This, though common, need not be so. An alternative method does, in fact, have distinct advantages.

The charging of actual expenses is usually parallel with the budgeted expense flow. With salary expense this usually means that each department is charged with its actual salaries. While this approach makes a lot of financial sense, it can create problems in personnel administration. To illustrate, let us make certain personnel-related assumptions. It is reasonable to say that:

1. Employees are employees of the company, not of individual departments. As such, they should be treated uniformly, regardless of the department they work in.

2. Transfer of salaried employees among departments is desirable to fill vacancies, build company experience, and prepare for career advancement.

3. Preestablished department budgets should not suffer because of salary changes or personnel transfers dictated by overall company policy or by overall company necessity.

4. Supervisors should not be budget-motivated to act against company personnel policy.

Now let us consider some specific actions that can readily circumvent these desirable aims:

• The supervisor of a branch office has been hit with an unbudgeted rise in heating costs. To help offset it, he defers all salary increases for six months. His employees are now falling behind, and as a result dissatisfaction arises.

• The supervisor of Department A has an opening for a secretary. However, she rejects the proposed transfer of candidate Smith from another department because Smith is "too high in the range" and would "cost too much," upsetting her budget. As a result Smith is debarred from a promising career.

• Department B happens to have a preponderance of older employees who are high in their range. The supervisor complains that this skew, which is beyond his control, makes his costs look high compared with other departments. He encourages employees to take early retirement, a chancy business.

• The supervisor of Department C has a large staff of nonexempts. She encourages high turnover in order to keep the group close to starting rates and thus hold her costs well below budget. As one result, the work is of poor quality.

• Owing to an organization change, Jones, an old supervisor, no longer has a job. Rather than let Jones go, you'd like to put him in Department E as a "coordinator," without cutting his pay. "Oh, no," says the supervisor of Department E. "I'd like to have him, but with his red-circle pay he'd wreck my budget." What do you do with Jones?

All these problems arise because supervisors are being charged with, and are focusing on, actual salaries. A simple way out is to charge them, not with actual salaries but with the standard (or midpoint) salaries of the positions filled.

This course follows a pattern similar to the standard-cost method of charging manufacturing departments with the cost of direct materials. Since supervisors cannot as a rule control the price of direct materials, their departments are customarily charged with the actual *quantity* used at a *standard* price. Thus any cost variance resulting from a change in price falls into a purchasing account, not the supervisors' departmental accounts. And any cost variance arising from usage, or yield, is properly isolated in the supervisors' departmental accounts (at the standard price).

Similarly, salary payroll at *actual* cost may be recorded in a central company account. This account is credited, and the

Figure 28. Standard-cost method of charging expenses.

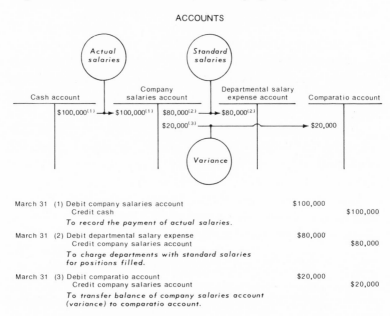

ACCOUNTS

March 31   (1) Debit company salaries account $100,000
           Credit cash $100,000
           To record the payment of actual salaries.

March 31   (2) Debit departmental salary expense $80,000
           Credit company salaries account $80,000
           To charge departments with standard salaries
           for positions filled.

March 31   (3) Debit comparatio account $20,000
           Credit company salaries account $20,000
           To transfer balance of company salaries account
           (variance) to comparatio account.

departmental accounts are debited, for the number of positions filled at the *standard* salary of each (see Figure 28). The departmental budgets, too, are constructed on the basis of standard salaries. The result is to hold the supervisor accountable for the number of positions filled, but not for salary levels—which are a matter of company policy. The central account picks up variances arising from any difference between actual and standard salary versus budget. This can be identified as a "comparatio" account. The departmental accounts display variances attributable only to staffing.

The comparatio account provides a measure, when compared with the total debits to the departmental salary account, of the extent to which the payroll is running over or under midpoints. Ideally, the account would run a credit balance at the beginning of the year. As the year progresses, the entries would shift to the debit side: the comparatio is moving over 1.00.

This procedure serves two purposes. First, it pinpoints accountability for salary variances, distinguishing between those arising from salary levels and those caused by overstaffing or understaffing. Second, it relieves the supervisor of the temptation to bend company salary policy in order to solve departmental problems.

PROBLEMS AND RISKS

Beyond the pure headache of having to do budgets at all lie a few difficulties that can arise in planning budgets and following up. Most of these stem from the disparity between warm expectations at budget time and cold reality in the ensuing year.

Overoptimism. Overoptimism on revenues may lead to overoptimism on the salary budget. Then, if revenues do not meet the forecast, you are unable to cover all your fixed overhead. If last-minute attempts at correction entail a reduction in predicted salary increases, you are in personnel trouble.

Ignoring Guidelines. The salary budget should agree with your guidelines for increases. If the budget is based on rough estimates of 5 percent increases and the guidelines for merit, tenure, and range adjustment increases provide for 8 percent, unexpected variances may pop up as the year progresses. Once again, corrective efforts may lead to inequities and grievances. Therefore, if the salary budget calls for stringencies, it is well to get revised guidelines in effect promptly so that outlays will not persist at a rate incompatible with budget objectives. Conversely, if the budget reliably portends prosperity, with an accompanying ability to support competitive salaries, the guidelines should be revised upward as necessary.

Padding. As noted above, it is not uncommon for some supervisors to budget for unfilled positions. These may be either positions formerly filled and now temporarily vacant or new positions that the supervisor proposes to add to the payroll. In either case, these empty slots should be carefully reviewed as a possible source of budget reduction. It is not uncommon for supervisors to list unfilled positions merely as a protection in case of emergency, with no intention of filling them.

Understaffing. The opposite of padding is understaffing—failing to budget for the additional salaried personnel that will be needed for proposed expansions of operation. When budgeted increases in revenue are contingent on opening a new department, adding to supervisory, sales, and professional resources, or going to a second or third shift, the salary budget should certainly include the added obligations. Often only top management has the overview needed to foresee such changes; department heads have a narrower outlook. Moreover, only at the top can there be assurance that optimistic sales estimates are not falling through to the bottom line without budgeted allowances for the people to (for example) write up the orders.

Publicity. Unintended disclosure of the salary budget can lead to trouble. Budgets, to be sure, need some publicity. No one can work within a budget without knowing what the budget is. At the same time, salary budgets can be a sensitive issue. If it becomes generally known that the salary budget is predicated on workforce reductions or additions—that changes in the organization are an integral part of its assumptions—morale is bound to get the shakes. Disclosure of the line-by-line budgeting of individual salaries can be especially troublesome. Employees infer that the budgeted increases—estimated though they may be—are locked-in certainties. For all these reasons, some firms find it advisable to keep the salary budget confidential and separate from other financial controls.

Incompleteness. There are a number of ways in which a salary budget may be made to look smaller than it really is. This can lead to surprises later on if unplanned expenses drive net profit below the budgeted level. Accordingly, the salary budget should be carefully screened to make sure that it includes all possible expenses that act like salaries but that are typically called something else. Salaried overtime pay is a good example. If it is apt to occur, it should be included in the budget.

Also, substitutions should not be overlooked. Attempts to achieve seeming reductions in salary costs, for budgeting purposes, encompass such stratagems as the use of part-time or temporary employees in lieu of full-time heads on the payroll and the use of hourly paid leaders instead of salaried supervisors. These are perfectly legitimate, and often desirable, measures. The point is to identify them.

11: SALARY CONTROL

SALARY CONTROL MONITORS and directs your salary program so that the program will work as you wish it to. Through fairly simple checks, it answers the following questions:

- Is salary practice adhering to company policy?
- Is it dealing fairly with the employees?
- Is it meeting the company's needs for getting and holding a productive workforce?
- Is it operating at a reasonably competitive cost?
- Is it staying within the law?

NEED FOR CONTROL

Control is needed because salary practice should never be taken for granted. For one thing, as we saw in Chapter 1, an increasingly large percentage of the nation's employees are in salaried positions. Salary cost is a growing contributor to the value of gross national product. It is probably no negligible fraction of your own company's total expense bill.

Not only do salaries bulk large in the cost picture; they are also more difficult to deal with than direct hourly labor costs. The latter tend to be variable. If production rises, so do they; if it falls, they fall likewise. Even indirect hourly labor is subject to ups and downs. But salaries tend to be fixed. Unless you have an unusual arrangement, a one-month sag in your business activity will not be matched by a corresponding decline in your salary payroll. That payroll cruises right along at its normal level as unabsorbed overhead.

Even when company economics seem to demand a paring of the salary payroll, the actual whittling down is difficult to achieve. A layoff of hourly employees is not unusual. But to pry a few valuable employees from the salary ranks—this is a real emotional nightmare for the supervisors who must do it.

One more thing: salary creep is insidious and almost invisible. You probably give a contracted wage increase periodically to your hourly union. You know exactly how much the increase is and when it occurs. No mystery about it. But if you strew salary increases throughout the year, the individual dollars can, in the absence of controls, slowly build to a greater total than ever anticipated. Like snowflakes, they just never amount to much at any one time. But they accumulate.

Beyond cost questions, salary administration has a direct effect on morale, on performance, on behavior, on company climate, and on your ability to build and sustain a productive corps of employees. Unless you check its fairness and equity now and then, your organization can be afflicted with a general malaise that is not readily diagnosed.

Not only must you control—that is, guide and follow up—to preserve internal soundness. You must also control to be sure that you are operating within the law and within the requirements of the various agencies that interpret and administer the law. No great problems should arise in meeting wages and hours standards—provided that you properly recognize nonexempt status and pay overtime when warranted. The tricky areas are those of EEO compliance. Here you are in a gray and changing legal environment. What has always seemed customary, reasonable, and justifiable to you may turn out to be an unwitting violation of the principles of nondiscrimination. Even aside from the law, you don't want to treat any class of employees unfairly. But the time and cost of legal processes add an economic imperative to that of fair play. It behooves you to institute controls that will hold you and your employees safe from challenge.

No single control method can answer all your requirements. From what amounts to a buffet of techniques, however, you can select those that do. Some you will want to use periodically, perhaps every month. Others serve their purpose only as special, once-in-a-while checks to be sure that things are as they should be.

BUDGETS

The most obvious control is, of course, the salary budget. Most companies have a budget, and in that budget most have an account that says "Salaries."

Of budgets, there are two kinds: fixed and flexible. The fixed budget posits one expected level of revenue and expenses for the year, based on a given level of business. The flexible budget provides graduated amounts of expense for various possible amounts of revenue associated with differing levels of business activity.

If, with the fixed budget, you find that your actual salary total varies from budget, you have to consider a number of possibilities. One is that your business level is not what you expected. "Salaries running higher than budget? Oh, yes, we had to put on a second shift last October." Easy explanation.

The flexible budget allows you to dig a little deeper. It predicts what your salary total should be if you have to add that second shift or put on two more clerks when orders exceed a predetermined level. Now when you have a variance you can sort out causes a little more thoroughly: Were three rather than two clerks added? Or have salary increases been swelling the payroll faster than you foresaw when you developed your flexible budget?

In any case, comparing actual with budgeted salaries tells you whether your overall salary cost is in control. And it's a good idea to compare every month. Nothing is worse than having to hold back on increases that are due in the latter part of the year because you handed out too much in the early months.

AUDITS

Comparison of actual with budgeted payroll tells you whether salaries are running along the course you laid out at the beginning of the year. But it does not answer the question of whether the actual charges are correct. This the audit can do. However an audit is performed—regularly or randomly, thoroughly or, shall we say, "samplingly"—here are a few points that it should cover.

Job Descriptions. Do the job descriptions describe what is actually being done by the reported incumbents? Often job changes are not recorded. Then both the description and the associated evaluation are out of date. For example, in the past your quality control clerk had to be able to compute standard deviations. But now this is done with a desk calculator. The clerk is only copying figures. Perhaps the job should be redescribed and reevaluated.

Job Assignment. It shouldn't happen, but it does: a supervisor turns someone in on a job other than the one performed. Such misreporting may be an out-and-out attempt to overpay. But it can also arise from a mistaken job number, a confusion about titles ("You mean there's a difference between steno-typist and steno-clerk?"), failure to change the title of an employee who has been transferred, or failure to get a new job defined ("Well, project engineer was the closest title I could find to what she's doing"). Such situations can be discovered only by inspection or interview.

Salary. Through clerical error (and nothing else, we hope) an employee may receive a salary other than that authorized for the job performed. This is not to say that the salary is merely out of range. Rather it is out of range without having had formal approval from an authorized person. The discrepancy can be identified by comparing actual salaries with those approved on salary action notices. (An example of such a notice is presented later in this chapter.)

Overtime. Time sheets should be checked to be sure that nonexempt employees are receiving any overtime pay for which they are eligible. In fact, checks should be made regularly to make sure that overtime is being entered on the time sheets. For one reason or another, employees sometimes feel that they should not record it.

Increases. Individual salary increases should conform to your guidelines. Thus promotional increases should not be granted unless warranted. Merit increases should correspond in percentage and timing to the rules established. Deviations should be few and only as authorized by a suitably high authority.

Real People. An audit should, of course, verify that each pay check is issued to a real, living employee of the company. (It is a good idea to make a similar verification of pension checks too.)

Files. Personnel history records should be reviewed to be sure that they are complete and up to date on jobs held, appraisals, and salary actions.

SURVEYS

Salary surveys are a kind of control. Through them you can make sure that you are maintaining whatever competitive salary position your policy calls for. Surveys tell you (1) how your benchmark jobs (and hence your salary curves) compare with those in other companies; (2) how much of a curve adjustment other employers are making; and (3) whether any positions are commanding out-of-line salaries because of supply–demand factors.

Surveys may include a wide range of intelligence, ranging from formal communications to the trade gossip that your employees hear.

COMPARATIO

You should track your comparatio monthly. For this purpose a simple graph suffices, as shown in Figure 29. In the illustration, it is assumed that your range (or curve) adjustment occurs in August. At that time you move all the midpoints up. As a result, your comparatio looks relatively low. Throughout the year, you grant increases. By the time July

Figure 29. Annual comparatio.

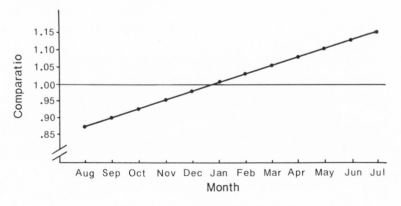

rolls around, your comparatio looks relatively high. If the same thing has happened in other companies, you and they will probably be moving your midpoints up the following August. The cycle repeats.

If your comparatio does not follow the general upward trend of Figure 29, you should know why. Some of the reasons for a low or high comparatio—such as high or low turnover or failure to follow guidelines for increases—were mentioned in earlier chapters.

Suppose the line rises much more steeply than in the diagram. Is this due to some internal malfunction? Or is it because a hot economy has forced you to give higher-than-planned increases? What is the effect on your budget?

If you have several salary curves—say, one for salespeople, one for "local" positions, one for professionals, and one for managers—you will want to track the comparatio for each. Is any group falling behind or getting too far ahead?

Further breakdowns of comparatio can also be useful. For example, departmental comparatios tell you if salary levels in any parts of the establishment are out of line with those in others. A department with a high comparatio may be headed for budget overruns. On the other hand, it may be full of senior employees or of professionals in high demand. You ought to know why.

The comparatio is also a good EEO check. Is the comparatio lower for blacks than for whites or lower for females than for males? Say your establishment is a college, and you have both male and female associate professors. If the females have a lower comparatio than the males, you have prima facie evidence of discrimination. It may well be that the females are lower only because they are relatively new on the job, while the males have been gathering increases for years. The question now is: Why are they so new? This the comparatio cannot tell you. But it can alert you to possible problem areas.

RATIOS

A number of easily calculated ratios and measures can give you a feel for salary trends in your company. These include year-to-year changes in the following.

Number of Salaried Employees. Month-to-month ratios of the total salaried employee population show whether your salaried force is advancing faster than your volume of business justifies. Sometimes a great leap forward is okay. In threshold companies—small, owner-managed companies making the transition to larger, professionally managed organizations—there is usually some point at which a quantum jump has to occur. In addition, intensified effort on quality, product development, or territorial expansion may require expansion of personnel a year or so in advance of profit feedbacks.

Salary Cost as a Percentage of Sales. This ratio should be watched carefully. As it rises, fixed expenses can eat up any advance in potential profits. Figure 30 illustrates a case calling for some concern. In the illustration salary cost as a percentage of sales is rising faster than profits, which have, in fact, shown a decline. Perhaps a tighter control on salaries would have prevented erosion of profits.

Supervisor–Employee Ratio. If this shows marked change from year to year, you should ask why. If it goes up, what does the business have to show for the increase? If it goes down, is any damage being done by too-thin supervision? The ratio is worth checking departmentally too. Empire builders

Figure 30. Salary cost versus profit as a percentage of sales.

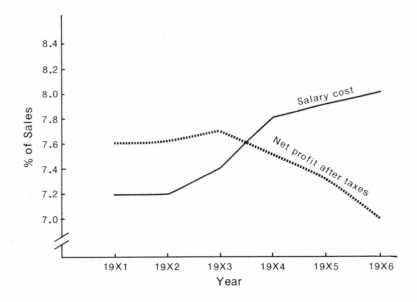

have a way of setting up multiple levels of supervision that cost money and create networks of unnecessary order passing.

Exempt–Nonexempt Ratio. This is worth following up, especially if you are under the impression that the new computer will pay for itself in clerical savings.

Average Evaluated Points per Position. If this ratio creeps up, something is happening to your organization. Either higher-level professional and managerial positions are being added or existing jobs are being reevaluated higher as a form of covert pay increase. But you'll never know what has happened if you don't have a control measure.

Key Salary Costs. It's not a bad idea to track your salary levels against key economic indicators, such as price trends, surveyed salary trends, and your own profitability movement. To do so you can't use total average salary per employee, for this is affected by changing job mix and employment level. You can, however, accumulate each year the average salary of a selected, fairly permanent group of benchmark jobs and use this as an ongoing measure. Graphing the results against economic or financial indexes provides a quick picture of annual correlation.

In Figure 31, for example, average key salaries, cost of liv-

Figure 31. Average salary versus trends.

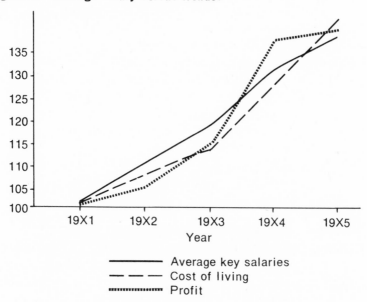

ing, and profit are graphed as index numbers, with 19X1 as the base year. The graph discloses that profit in the last year has flattened alarmingly after a steep rise. But perhaps this is not too bad; the year before was unusually high—you took price increases, no doubt. The line for average key salaries, however, has lost some of its upward momentum. And the cost-of-living line is climbing faster than either. Apparently, you are facing salary pressures next year. The question is: What effect will increases have on that profit plateau?

Average Percentage Increase. Let's say that you have excellent written guidelines for various types of salary increases. But are they being adhered to? One way to find out is to add up all the increase percentages—those for merit, let us say— and divide by the total number of positions filled. From this you get an average merit increase per employee position. If you track percentage increases month by month as the year progresses, you can see if you are holding on course.

Two things you don't do. First, you don't divide by the total number of employees, because turnover could make this number unrepresentatively high. Second, you don't divide total increase dollars by total salaries at the start of the year, because this understates the effect of increases given in the later months. Like some of the other controls, this one can be used as a check on individual departments and on classes of employee. And in the EEO arena, it can tell you if protected classes are getting as good a percentage as others.

RED CIRCLES

Red-circle situations should be reviewed periodically. It is a temptation, once someone has been put on a red-circle salary, to think that a problem has been solved. But has it? With a red-circle salary, you are paying more for a position than your salary system specifies. Some part of your business is too costly. At the same time, you have not eliminated unhappiness. Other employees see the red-circle incumbent as someone who is either miscast or (they suspect) overpaid in comparison with themselves. As for the incumbent, he or she will in all likelihood receive no salary increases until the ranges catch up with the red-circle pay. Not happy. No motivation. Nowhere to go. Beached.

At least once a year the red-circle list should be examined to see if any opportunities have arisen to reassign its members to jobs more in line with their pay levels—or to jobs that would put them on a track with a better future. If you want to go all out, you might even have a talk with the incumbents. How do they feel about their position? Do they have any ideas? What would they like to do? But, you say, all this was discussed when their red-circle status was established. And how could they be dissatisfied when they're overpaid compared with everyone else? Talk to them anyway. Maybe something has changed in the meantime.

Even when a red circle exists because you had to exceed range to hire a high-priced star in a competitive market, some communication is a good idea. Does this person, knowing his or her special status, have any questions about future security? Is that competitive market beginning to look attractive again?

POSITION CONTROL

Salaried positions, once filled, are difficult to eliminate. Whatever is being done in these positions usually turns out to be a convenience, even a necessity, that cannot be dispensed with. The best way to keep salaried costs down is to erect barriers to the addition of salaried employees. One way to do so is through position control.

A position control system begins with a list of authorized positions and the number of employees needed to fill them. For example, one line on such a list might be:

Dept. No.	Dept. Name	Job No.	Job Title	Authorized Incumbents
604	Purchasing	1008	Expeditor	3

The system also includes "rules of the game." For example:

- The position control list shall not exceed the budget.
- No vacancy shall be refilled without written assurance from the supervisor that the duties are (1) still necessary and (2) impossible to reassign.
- No staffing beyond the authorized number of incumbents shall occur without written authorization from the president.
- No new positions shall be created without written authorization from the president.

Though these proscriptions may seem excessively bureaucratic, they are essential for salary control. They may indeed be compared with the safeguards surrounding additions to capital equipment. Cost-conscious establishments make no outlay for capital equipment without a payoff-oriented appropriation. What will the proposal cost? What benefits will flow from it? How long will it take for these benefits to repay the investment? One year? Two? Fifteen? What is the discounted cash flow rate of return on the outlay (the DCF–ROI)? As a rule, funds are not committed unless the investment will yield a higher rate of return than any other use of the funds.

Consider now the addition of a position to the salaried payroll. The proposed salary is $15,000 a year. But with fringes and the associated expenses of supplies, telephone, and office services, the total cost is closer to $25,000 a year. In five years this position will have cost some $125,000. And this does not include salary increases. Why, the new position demands as much cash as many an asset!

As a matter of financial prudence, you should test this proposal as rigorously as one for a new asset. The new position should be self-liquidating. It should pay for itself through either addition to profits or avoidance of potential loss of profits. Even in a nonprofit institution, the effect on the overall expense–revenue ratio cannot be overlooked. The best way to accomplish these ends is through a written "people appropriation" request setting forth the proposal, the benefits, and the payback.

An example of such a request is shown in Figure 32. On its face, the proposal looks pretty good: five-year cash inflows with a present value of $501,457 against five-year cash outlays with a present value of $152,451. The mere existence of the position control process acts to restrict such undertakings to those that have business merit. It focuses attention on the cumulatively high costs of salaries and the need for some reciprocity between salaries and company income. Your only question, if confronted with such a proposal, might be: "Why can't we do this with the people we have?" But the process will doubtless have led your petitioner to anticipate the question and supply you with a convincing answer.

If the creation of new positions deserves scrutiny, so does the filling of vacancies. Too often it is assumed that the existence of a block on the organization chart is a priori sanction for keeping it occupied. If someone vacates it, a replacement is automatic. Not so.

Getting rid of—even recognizing—superfluous positions is difficult when people are sitting in them. But when, through

Figure 32. "People appropriation" request.

> ### NEW POSITION
>
> *Proposal:*   It is proposed to establish the position of mate-
> rials manager.
>
> *Benefits:*   By instituting and operating programs for bet-
> ter management of materials, the new position
> will effect the following annual savings in
> today's dollars:
>
> | | | |
> |---|---|---:|
> | Inventory reduction carrying charges | | $ 30,000 |
> | Yield improvement | | 100,000 |
> | Scrap sales | | 5,000 |
> | | Total | $135,000 |
>
> *Costs:* | | | |
> |---|---|---:|
> | Estimated salary | | $ 22,000 |
> | Fringes | | 6,600 |
> | Office overhead | | 11,000 |
> | | Total | $ 39,600 |
>
> *Results:*   Benefits—Present value over five
> years with 6% annual inflation
> and 15% discounting factor $501,457
>
> Costs—Present value with 8%
> annual escalation and 15% dis-
> counting factor $152,451

transfer, promotion, or resignation, a position becomes vacant, this is an opportune time to submit it to a test of necessity. What will happen if the position is not refilled? Can a
change in systems or procedures permit its functions to be
performed more efficiently? Are the functions still necessary?
Can the duties be split up among other positions? Is anyone
else already performing the same or related functions?

Suppose the inventory clerk in the factory is promoted.

Upon checking, you find that inventory records are now also available from the computer file in the accounting department. No replacement. The vice president of sales resigns to work in a larger company. You set up a combination job, vice president of sales and marketing, for your existing marketing vice president, thus getting more effective control and eliminating a friction point. No replacement. In each case, a reduction of fixed expenses.

These examples may seem like contemptible cheese paring. In an expanding company they may even seem inappropriate. But an expanding company is the very one that will attract the attention of competitors. Only by carving a low-cost profile, and freeing funds for marketing thrust, can you prepare to fend them off. And being reluctant to fill vacancies is one of the more painless forms of cost reduction.

You are well justified in operating a position control system. It helps to prevent an obese payroll. It relieves you of having to be a Solomon on every proposal for a new position, because it enlists the proposer, through cost–benefit analysis, in the commitment to company objectives. By putting a check on staff expansion, it maintains funding for adequate payment of the employees you have. And certainly there is no point in having all sorts of controls, rules, and guidelines on salary levels and merit increases unless you have equally effective controls on the number of employees who receive them.

APPROVALS

A further form of control is supplied by an adequate approval system. Salary actions are influenced by emotional bias, personal pressures, confusion of individual employee needs with company welfare, mistaken data, narrow outlooks, witless generosity, and simple fraud. A salary increase can be a reward or a bribe. Failure to give an increase can be

Figure 33. Salary action form.

SALARY ACTION

| Name | Clock No. | Position | Pos. No. |

| Department | Dept. No. | Effective Date |

Nature of Change

☐ Transfer ☐ Promotion ☐ Merit Increase ☐ Reclassification
☐ Hire ☐ Range Adjustment Increase ☐ Other (explain below)

Change Is ☐ Within Guidelines ☐ Outside Guidelines*
☐ Within Position Control ☐ Over Position Control*

	Date	Job Title	Job Grade	Increase $	Increase %	New Salary	% of Midpoint
Next-to-last increase							
Last increase							
Proposed increase							

Last Appraisal Date _____

Reasons for Change:

Line Approvals _____ _____ _____ _____
                Full name   Date   Full name   Date

Personnel Review _____ _____
                  Full name   Date

*President _____ _____
            Full name   Date

a warning or an act of revenge. Every salary action should be seen by at least two pairs of eyes (in addition to those of the recipient).

For control, then, you should have a written record accompanied by suitable approvals. For this purpose, a simple form may be used (see Figure 33). Typical approval requirements include:

1. Hiring salaries up to $XX require prior approval of both the line supervisor and personnel manager. Those above $XX also require approval of the president.

2. Salary increases within guidelines require approval of two levels of line supervision. Those for salaries in excess of $XX per year require approval of the president.

3. Salary increases outside guidelines require approval of the personnel manager and the president.

4. Salary decreases require approval of the personnel manager and the president.

5. Additions to the position control list, refilling of vacant positions, and demotions require prior approval of the president.

Although written approvals may seem to impose a heavy burden on the president, the fact that the approvals are required will probably act to suppress their number.

RECORDS

The salary action for each employee is, of course, made part of the permanent record. An easy way to do so is to file the salary action notices under the employee's name. At the same time, for ease in reference, the key figures may be transcribed to a summary card or a computer tape.

12: THE SALARY ETHIC

ALTHOUGH SALARY MANAGEMENT seems to be concerned with matters of policy and procedure—surveys, evaluations, increases, and the like—these are but the gates and switches, so to speak, of a larger system called the Distribution of Wealth. What the company really is doing is allocating resources. In fact, the establishment is rather like a giant pinball machine. Money shoots into the top of the machine, and part of management's job is to guide it to the right pocket. The question is: Which pocket is right?

Now as soon as we use the word "right" we get into something a little more abstract than pinball machines or, for that matter, salary systems. We get into economics, ethics, and perhaps morals. These are the areas that deal with right and entitlement and especially, in our concern for salaries, with questions of who should get how much. In the pinball machine analogy, these are the guiding disciplines that govern the design of your company's overall flow of marbles—in this case, its cash flow.

You may not think of cash flow as a matter of ethics. Yet whenever there is to be a discretionary apportionment of dollars to one or another "pocket," something very like ethics comes into play. No, you say, not ethics. Only hardheaded business necessities dictate decisions on where to lodge the money that bounces around the company. But how do you evaluate the degree of necessity and the outcomes it may lead you to choose? By what standards?

ALTERNATIVES FOR ALLOCATING PROFITS

Given a choice, should what a business earns over and above its bare survival needs go to the owners, to employees, or to internal investment?

For the sake of an example, let us imagine a least-cost business. It prices what it sells as high as the market will bear for that volume which maximizes total revenue. It pays just enough for materials, labor, and overhead to support a level of quality that will hold its customers. It spends just as much on marketing and sales as will sustain its market share. And it pays its salaried force just enough to keep positions filled. In comes an annual profit. This is the return on the investment in the business.

Now, then, the CEO looks at this profit picture and, in planning for the future of the enterprise, asks: Should this profit and its associated rate of return be altered in any way?

Once the CEO gets past a few going-in assumptions—that the firm is solvent, meets government requirements, is not wholly union-dominated, and does not have a monopoly—he has choices of where to put the money. For example, some of the company's money, above or below the profit line as the case may be, may be allocated to:

- Higher pay or benefits for hourly workers.
- Investment in new product development.
- Spending to build market share.
- Price reduction to give customers a break.
- Accumulation of surplus cash for a future acquisition.
- Maximum possible dividends to shareholders.
- Higher salaries for everybody.

- Higher salaries for the management-executive-professional group only.

Not an alternative in this example is investment in cost-reducing facilities. Per our assumption, the CEO is already running a least-cost business. We're talking about money left over *after* taking care of needs for the present business. To which of the foregoing "pockets" should it be guided? However much goes to one, so much the less goes to any other. Let us consider each in turn.

More for Hourly Workers

Voluntarily and unilaterally raising the pay of hourly workers just because profits permit doesn't seem like a real-world possibility. If there is a union, it has already negotiated rates as high as the company need go. If there isn't, the company is probably paying as much anyway in order to keep a union out. So just shoving more compensation at hourly workers does not offer a lot of attraction to our CEO.

Investment in New Products

A CEO who listens to proponents of product life-cycle theories is going to feel a compulsion to spend some of the money on new product development. Not to do so is virtually to align oneself with the flat-earth club. But while the essentiality of new products is part of today's business credo, finding facts to support it is difficult. In the grocery industry, for example, some 5,000 new products are offered every year—and a typical store carries only about 10,000 products to begin with. This might lead one to say, regardless of what industry one is in: "Everybody's doing it so it must make sense." Yet those in the know say that only about 2 percent of the products developed survive. These aren't very good odds. They don't come near the odds of rolling snake eyes—and responsible CEOs wouldn't risk company money on the dice table, would they?

Still, new product development is the thing to do. Maybe the CEO feels that some of the money has to go into it. Though it doesn't on the average seem to be too rewarding, it's the only game in town.

But those odds—they do raise an ethical question, don't they? Even with the best of intentions, should a CEO gamble with the company bankroll at someone else's expense?

Spending to Build Market Share

Spending to increase market share doesn't seem like a bad idea, especially if you listen to your advertising agency. Some advocates of portfolio management see the journey to higher share as the hajj that every true believer with a profitable product is bound to make. But it has its *buts.* For one thing, how do your competitors feel about your share growth? If they undertake retaliatory spending, that Mecca you were heading toward may turn out to be a black hole into which your dollars tumble, never to be seen again. Oh, sure, some of the beverage people and auto people and TV people have succeeded with share growth. So may any company. But it takes money. Does the CEO's charter justify risking that money, which could have gone elsewhere?

Price Reduction

To reduce prices (or forgo increases under inflation) is always an alternative for the solvent business. The altruistic business executive, of whom there are still quite a few, sees it as a blessing to hard-pressed customers and an aspirin for a febrile economy. The strategic business executive sees it as a means to build volume, thereby spreading overhead absorption, expanding market share as a nest egg for future profits, and incidentally protecting jobs. The cautious executive, however, sees it as a possible first smoke signal in a price war, luring the industry into what historians call intestine strife, which can bring only sorrow to the company and its employees.

Strangely, then, price reduction—that seemingly dollars-and-cents affair—is implicated with cloudy good and evil as much as with stark finance. Are the long-range best interests of consumers served when you drop bombs in an otherwise stable marketplace? Is it ethical to take price actions that may force other companies and their employees out of business?

Future Acquisition

One thing the CEO and the board of directors can do with any spare dollars lying around is quietly set them aside for the future acquisition of another business. In doing so, they have to remember that the scent of all this bread in the larder may attract ravenous predators who will gobble up their own company. Assuming this doesn't happen, there is then the prospect of adopting new members into the corporate family, with the unarguable benefits of diversification, growth potential, and portfolio balancing. Still, the process is not foolproof. Why else has the business world experienced acquisitions, purchased at such a premium as to shrivel rates of return, being dissolved because they were unmanageable or quietly traded off again at a loss? Something went wrong and a hemophilia of money was the result.

We look at these questions, not in criticism of what is common practice, but to call attention to a trend in board of directors' prerogatives—that of investing shareholders' money instead of paying it out in dividends that the shareholders can reinvest for themselves.

Well, says the CEO (for after all, it is he and not the board who is probably the chief huntsman), why not? It *is* risk capital, isn't it? So there's a risk. And better that it be invested in its entirety before passing through that IRS screen which filters half the substance out of dividends.

Certainly it's not unethical to invest someone else's money when you happen to have your hands on it. Besides, who earned the money? But there's at least an element of judgment that lies somewhere beyond the clear confines of day-to-day operations. Here's some money. Whom does it go to? Is this only a matter of who has readiest access to it? Or does "deserving" merit consideration?

Dividends

Yet another option is to direct available cash into dividends. This is not just a be-good-to-stockholders gift. It has potential reflexive effects on the business and its officers. Higher dividends may pump up the stock price. The shares then have added glitter as trading chips in exchange for an acquisition. Good for the business. Not only that. With a higher price the stock may also have more value to those who hold options. Good for the officers.

On the other hand, are those stockholders entitled to a full slice of the pie? They're already getting a return on their investment that the market, in its wise determination of stock price, has appraised as satisfactory. What did *they* do to build profits? Why not distribute money around inside the business, where it was earned and where it can do some real good? Why pass it along to outsiders, and worse, to the government, which will appropriate its second cut on the payout?

Salaried Employee Participation

Finally, and this is why we have discussed the subject in a book on salary management, money can flow, not into the aforementioned pockets but into salaries. Our starting assumption was that the salaried employees are being paid just enough to keep positions filled. And the company is solvent. So now the question is: Should they be the ones to receive a bigger piece of the pie?

In their favor it might be argued that to such extent as the company succeeds it is due to their efforts (as contrasted with that of the stockholders, for example). Therefore, in fairness, they ought to share in the company's success. Thou shalt not, says the Bible, muzzle the ox when it treads out the grain. Raise their salary levels. Raise the salary curve.

Now, the argument goes, with more disposable income, employees will have a greater sense of worth and responsibility. With abatement of personal financial pressures, they will be able to thrust greater energies into the conduct of the business. So what has been done in fairness also redounds to the welfare of the firm.

But wait. Many salaried jobs are merely procedural. In terms of job demand, the people who fill them are all but interchangeable. You have only to tell the incumbents the drill, and anyone who wears shoes can do the job. Paying more than the least you can get away with is, if anything, unfair to those employees who occupy more demanding, contributory positions.

No, the argument might continue, this isn't quite true. Even on the most routine jobs, it is how the work is performed that makes a company succeed. Well-paid, participating, ungrudging employees notice things that need doing, go out of their way to do things right, make small improvements, help each other, think of the company's interests. This sort of path clearing at lower levels is what permits the creativity and professional expertise of the upper levels to drive the company forward. In fact, it is the lower-level "civil service" that keeps the company alive through the constant change of actors in executive ranks that is so characteristic of today's industry.

But no, the argument might proceed, it is the professional-managerial-executive ranks that should be paid as much as can be wrung out of the books without actually injuring the lines of credit or stirring up the stockholders. Never mind the replaceable lower levels. It is the upper levels that conceive and carry out whatever measures keep the firm alive and (possibly) growing. They of all people deserve the returns. Indeed, through a sort of internal spoils system, they are the most eligible and opportunistic recipients.

NONPROFIT ESTABLISHMENTS

These various arguments, in more limited form, apply with equal stress to enterprises in which neither profit nor financial return on investment is an objective.

Thus of the money available to the administration of a religious sect, a union headquarters, a museum, a trade association, or a school system, allocations may be made to existing or new functions, to expansion of areas covered, to improved services, to better facilities, or to salaries. In the contrary direction, reduction of incoming revenue may be reflected in contraction of the amounts available to these accounts. In any case, how much to put where is just as much an issue in the nonprofit enterprise as it is in the profit-oriented establishment.

SUMMARY

Our original example postulated a business with an excess of funds faced with a choice of where to put the money. In reality, the choice exists under almost any conditions. True, a failing business has small option. When the furniture is being broken up to feed the furnace, who expects a comfortable seat? Employees are lucky not to get a *cut* in pay.

This exception aside, any going enterprise does have freedom of choice. And the decision on whether to move money into marketing, research, expansion, dividends, or salaries is made on the basis of an underlying, not always recognized, philosophy.

At one extreme is the view—favored in many schools of business today—that the only purpose of a company is to generate a high and growing return on investment. All other objectives are secondary and cannot in fact be realized unless the first is kept paramount.

At the other extreme is the philosophy, seldom voiced but not unknown to practice, that the purpose of a business is to create joy, of all things, for its customers and participants. This it does by selling that which people recognize as a desirable benefit, by rewarding its investors with the return that induced them to invest, and by affording to its employees the highest salary levels compatible with business continuity.

Now, of course, there are the in-between views as well. Most companies, no doubt, try to hit a reasonable balance among all claimants.

But in the management of salaries the decision is in the end one of ethics: What is the *right* thing to do? Even to interpret "right" as something to be measured only in financial terms is a decision that falls in the domain of ethics. Other measures exist as well.

In the management of salaries, then, more than the simple application of procedures must be considered. You may well ask if your company is using its money in a way that makes both business and ethical sense. Should salaries be held on the low side in order to free funds for other purposes? Should they be raised as high as possible in order to create a company Shangri-La in the commercial wilderness? Should salary largesse be distributed broadside to everybody in a humanistic orgy of benevolence, or should it fall neatly into the hands of those who control it? All this is something to think about.

And it introduces considerations not encountered in the purely monetary calculus of business classes. In every organization a salary ethic is at work, perceived or not by those whom it affects.

INDEX

advances, 10, 167, 175
American Association of Museums, 104
American Bankers Association, 104
American Institute of Industrial Engineers, 104
American Management Associations, 104
annual increase, 85
    see also periodic increases
appraisals, 141–157
    characterized, 142
    criticisms of, 144–145, 152–153
    formality in, 142–143
    see also employee performance appraisal; job evaluation
assessment, 142
assessment centers, 142
audits, 209–210

Bacon, Sir Francis, quoted, 94
basic salary
    characterized, 64, 70, 78–79
    job evaluation points in, 71
    in position ranking, 35–36
    salary curve plotting of, 71
    as salary range midpoint, 80, 87
    see also midpoint salary; minimum salary; standard salary
bell-curve distribution, in employee performance appraisal, 146–148, 155
benchmark jobs
    in job evaluation, 46–47
    in salary cost checkups, 215
    in salary rating, 160
bias
    in employee evaluation, 156
    in job evaluation, 51–52, 55
    see also discrimination
bonus, 116, 122
    merit increase vs., 92–93
    in out-of-line hiring, 95–96
    in salary surveys, 122
budget(s), 208–209
budget planning, 186–205
    characterized, 187
    comparatio in, 202–203
    costs vs. growth in, 188–189

budget planning (*cont.*)
  developmental, 202–203
  employee numbers in, 187,
    194, 199, 204
  forecasting in, 195–197
  by organizational systems
    analysis, 191–192
  padding vs. underestimating
    in, 204, 205
  payroll vs. revenues in, 188
  salaried force regulation in,
    188–192
  salary costs in, 192–195,
    203–204
  for salary increases, 195–201
  standard cost method in,
    200–203
  unit total salary method,
    198–199
  zero-base method in, 191
Bureau of Labor Statistics, 105,
  109, 192
business acquisitions, 228

cash flow, ethics of, 224
College Placement Council,
  104
company policy
  budgetary considerations in,
    187
  merit increases and, 166
  performance appraisal and,
    155–156
  on salaries, *see* salary policy
comparatio levels
  in budget planning, 202–203

definition and formula for,
  125–126, 131
in departmental operations,
  137–138
in discrimination (EEO)
  check, 212
high, factors in, 135–137,
  152
low, factors in, 132–134
performance appraisals and,
  152
in salary control, 211–213
in salary policy implementation, 127–128, 131–134,
  138–140
for specific salary levels,
  126–127, 131
time factor in, 127–129, 135,
  137
workforce size and, 132, 134,
  136
compensable job factors, 40–43
  see also job evaluation
competitive market position
  changes in, 140
  comparatio level indication
    of, 125–128, 131
  salary budgeting and, 192
  salary curve indication of,
    116–119
  salary payments levels and,
    9–10, 25–26, 120–123, 127
  salary surveys and, 100–103
consumer price index, 105,
  109, 192
cost-of-living allowances, 161
  in locality transfers, 175

merit increases vs., 162–164
  in salary survey data, 122

death, model salary payment
    at, 29
demotions, 27, 178–181, 223
  see also salary decrease
departmental operations
  budget planning and,
    200–203
  comparatio levels and,
    137–138, 140, 212
  performance ratings and,
    152
department head, promotion
    of, 36–38
disclosures
  of appraisals, unintentional,
    157
  of job ranking points, 60–62
  of salary information, 23–24,
    29, 69, 80, 163–164
  of salary budget plans,
    204–205
discrimination
  appraisals charged as,
    156–157
  comparatio levels as check
    on, 212
  EEO compliance and,
    156–157, 207, 208, 216
  in job evaluation, 51–52, 55
  by sex, 97, 212
diversification, corporate, 228
dividend distribution, 229
Dorfman, D. D., cited, 155

downgrading, model policy for,
    28

education, 50
employee(s), salaried
  audit of, 210
  in budget planning, 194, 199,
    204
  capabilities of, vs. job de-
    mands, 62, 155–156
  exempt to nonexempt, ratio
    of, 214
  immobile, 89
  job description writing by,
    32
  job evaluation by, 60–62
  job performance by, *see* em-
    ployee performance ap-
    praisal
  morale of, *see* employee
    moral
  new, 85, 165
  numbers of, 204, 213, 218
  profit allocation to, 229–231
  retention of, 88–90, 135–136
  supervisor ratio to, 213–214
  temporary, 191, 205
  in titled positions, 218
  turnover of, *see* employee
    turnover
  union vs. nonunion, 163
  see also hourly employees;
    workforce
employee morale
  red circle raises and,
    215–217

employee morale (*cont.*)
  salary administration and,
    207
  salary increases and, 181–182
employee performance ap-
    praisal
  characterized, 142
  checklist for, 146, 147
  criteria in assessing, 152–155
  criticism of process of,
    144–145
  formal approach in, 142–143
  legal vulnerability of,
    156–157
  merit increases and, 91, 93,
    141, 149–150, 165–166
  methods for, 145–148
  normal distribution in,
    '146–148, 155
  policy implications of,
    155–156
  on promotion, 168
  by supervisors, 141–157
  terminology in, 142
  timing of, 150–151
  training seminar for, 153
employee turnover
  aging in, 134
  in budget planning, 194, 199
  factors affecting, 89–90, 132
  low comparatio indication
    of, 132
ethics of salaries, 232–233
executive officer, salary deci-
    sion making role of, 1–8,
    12

experience
  evaluation points for, 50
  in salary range spread, 90–91

fixed budget, 208
flexible budget, 208
forced distribution, in em-
    ployee appraisal, 146–148
fringe benefits, 122
grievances, 65
guidelines, salary, 29
  adjustment of, 140, 184–185
  in budget planning, 203–204
  need for, 181

hiring, salaries on, 95–96
holiday pay, 10
hourly employees
  criteria for wages of, 2
  immediate supervisor salary
    overlap with, 83
  increases for, on transfer to
    salary, 174
  profit allocation to, 226
hourly wages, salaries vs., 2–5,
    206

increases in salary
  averaging, 216
  budget planning for,
    195–201
  company wide vs. individual,
    162–164
  comparatario levels and,
    138–140
  cost-of-living, 161–164

cost to company, *see* payroll
    costs
cost vs. productivity in, 158,
    160, 163
employee attitudes toward,
    159, 163–164
formal policy on, 10
general vs. merit, 163–164
for inflation, *see* inflation ad-
    justments
on job reevaluation, 176–177
lag in rate of, 134
merit vs. inflationary, 182
negative, 178–181
omitted, 183–184
overgenerous, 183
performance appraisals and,
    141–144, 149–152
performance vs., 159–160
periodic, 85, 86, 163–164
problems of, 181–185
progressive, 169–171, 193
on promotion, 27–28, 78,
    167–175
rules for, 84–85
as salary curve adjustments,
    161–164
temporary, 177–178
for tenure, 168–169
timing of, 162, 164
types of, 161
union and nonunion, 163
written approval of, 223
see also inflationary in-
    creases; merit increases;
    periodic increases; promo-
    tional increases

inflationary increases
general increases vs.,
    163–164
for living cost increases, *see*
    cost-of-living allowances
merit increases vs., 182
for red circle employees, 96
in salary budgeting, 192
salary curve adjustments for,
    101–102, 118–119, 122,
    128–129
in salary survey data,
    101–102, 122
time factor in, 127–129
Infosystems, 105, 108, 109
initiative, rating of, 43
interrupted service, 10
involuntary separations, 28–29

job analysts, job descriptions
    by, 31
job assignments, audit of,
    209–210
job descriptions
audits of, 209
in employee performance
    appraisal, 148
exaggeration of requirements
    in, 54–55
in job evaluation, 31, 33–35,
    49
reevaluation of, 28, 32, 209
in salary surveys, 106, 107,
    209
in training programs, 33, 97
uses for, 32–34
writing of, 31–32

job evaluation, 30–31
  benchmark positions in,
    46–47
  bias in, 51–52, 55
  in budget planning, 191
  by committees, 58–59
  compensable factors in,
    40–42
  cross checking in, 46
  definition of, 142
  disclosures in, 60–62
  education in, 50–51
  experience in, 50–51
  factor points in, 42–48
  flexibility in, 49–50
  job descriptions in, 31–35
  job importance vs., 31
  job ranking and, 35–40
  of modified jobs, 56
  in newly created positions,
    56
  purposes of, 30
  salary levels and, 30, 70–71
  salary range and, 64–66
  by specialists, 56–59
  title vs. responsibility in,
    52–53
  unionized employees and, 61
  see also job ranking; job re-
    evaluation
job markets
  budget planning and,
    192–193
  salary curves for, 71–72, 122
  salary surveys of, 102–103
  sudden changes in, 140

job performance
  experience and, 90
  evaluation of, 30–33
  job descriptions in rating,
    33–35
  low comparatio level vs.,
    134–135
  merit increases and, 65–66,
    91, 93, 141, 149–150
  salary range spread and,
    90–91
  terminology in, 142
  see also employee perform-
    ance appraisal
job ranking, 35–40
  base salaries in, 35–36
  bias test for, 55
  compensable factors in,
    40–43
  disclosure problems in,
    60–62
  factor points in, 42–46
  job evaluation and, 35–40
  judgment in, 38–39
  merit increases and, 91
  by promotional position,
    36–38
  revision pressure in, 61
  salary equivalents in, 59, 62
  salary level vs., 83
  see also job evaluation
job reevaluation
  corrective, 177, 209
  demotion following, 28,
    178–179
  maintenance of, 219–221

model salary policy for, 28
salary increases in, 176–177
job requirements, 26, 53, 62
job titles
  accountability vs., 52–53
  audit of, 209–210
  control of, 217–218
  cost analysis by, 218–219
  evaluation in terms of, 52
  mismatches with competitive, 121
  progressive, 169
  reevaluation of, 219–221
  replacement of, 219–221
  rule for numbers of holders of, 218
  in salary surveys, 106–108
jury duty pay policy, 10

knowledge, as compensable factor, 42–43

large companies, salary policies in, 4–11
level of absence, 10

market share building, 227
maximum salary, 79
  employee termination at, 182
  merit increases and, 165
  on promotion, 174
  see also red circle salaries
Mencius, quoted, 37
merit increases, 5, 87–88
  accumulated, 167–168

annual, 85
bonus vs., 92–93
budget planning for, 193
employee performance appraisals and, 141, 149–150
employee retention and, 89, 98
excessive, 136
general increases plus, 163–164
as lump-sum advances, 167
maximum salary and, 165
model policy for, 26, 28
motivation and, 94, 163
on promotion, 167–168, 174
salary growth effects of, 92–94
tenure and, 165, 168
timing of, 92, 166–168
midpoint salary
  in budget planning, 201–202
  characterized, 87–89
  inflationary adjustment of, 101–102
  salary curve plotting of, 71, 118
  in salary range, 78–80, 165
  see also basic salary; standard salary
military service pay policy, 10
minimum salary, 79
  basic salary vs., 80
  below, 55, 96–97, 165
  in grade, on promotion, 174
  new employees at, 85, 165
  policy on, 18, 165
  stretching out, 182

motivation, employee
  company policy and, 26
  merit increases as, 94, 163
  promise of increases as, 184

new employees, 85, 165
new product development,
  226–227
nonprofit organizations, 231
nonsalary payments, 122
nonunion employees, 163
normal distribution, in employee appraisal, 146–148,
  155

*Occupational Titles, U.S. Gov-
  ernment Dictionary of,* 41
occupations, comparatio levels
  by, 127
organization, authority vs., 53
organizational systems analysis,
  191–192
overhead value analysis, 191
overtime, audit of, 210
overtime pay policy, 10

part time employees, 191, 205
pay discrimination charges, 55,
  97
payroll costs
  audit of, 209–210
  in budget planning, 186–187,
    192–195, 208–209
  control of, 206–207; *see also*
    salary control
  economic indicators and,
    215–216

of individual vs. general increases, 163–164
of merit increases, 98, 166,
  167
profits vs., 215–216
red circle wages as, 215–217
reduction of, 207
salary dispersion and, 86
salary increases as, 158, 163
sales revenues vs., 188, 213
total expenses vs., 3–4,
  206–207
see also salaries; salary control
peak employment elimination,
  191
people appropriation request,
  219
performance, *see* employee
  performance appraisal; job
  performance
periodic increases, 85, 86, 88,
  163–164
personnel, numbers of, 187,
  210
personnel manager, 4
Pope, Alexander, quoted, 120
position control system,
  217–223
position ranking, 35–40, 46–47
  see also job ranking
price reduction, 227–228
probationary job pay, 10
productivity, 158–159
professional job upgrading,
  169–171
profit allocation, 225–231

progressive salary increases,
169–171, 193
promotions
characterization of, 70,
171–172, 174
hourly wage to supervisory,
78
job ranking of, 36–38
merit increases and,
167–168, 174
minimum, 80
model policy on, 26–28
overlapping pay ranges and,
98
performance appraisal and,
168
progressive, 169–171
salary grades and, 69–71
salary increases with, 27–28,
167–168, 174–175, 210
temporary, 28

raises, *see* increases in salary;
inflationary increases;
merit increases; periodic
increases
range adjustment increases,
131
recruitment
bonus pay on, 96
salary range expecta-
tions in, 95–96
red circle salaries, 66
justification for, 96
morale problems with,
215–217
payroll cost of, 215–217

range of, 25, 28, 201
systematic reassessment of,
217
relocation expenses, 103

salaried employees, *see* employees, salaried; work-
force
salaried positions, *see* job titles;
supervisors
salaries
actual vs. planned, 25,
124–125, 131, 134; *see also*
salary policy
audit of, 210
in budget planning, 188–205
compensable factors in,
40–46
ethics of, 232–233
formula for calculating, 72
fringe benefits and, 122
increases in, 158–160; *see
also* increases in salary
internal equity model for, 25
job qualifications and, 40
maximum, 79, 165, 174, 182
minimum, *see* minimum salary
policy for, *see* salary policy
profit allocation to, 229–231
range of, *see* salary range
red circle, 25, 28, 66, 96,
201, 215–217
salary curve of, *see* salary
curve
surveys of, *see* salary surveys

salaries (*cont.*)
total cash compensation vs., 106
see also basic salary; payroll costs
salary administration, *see* salary management
salary budget, *see* budget(s); budget planning; payroll costs
salary changes
compressive, 178-179, 182-183
formal policy on, 10
on locality transfer, 175-176
see also increase in salary; merit increases
salary control
approval system for, 221-223
budgets in, 208-209; *see also* budget planning
comparatio in, 211-213
functions of, 206-207
of job grading, 214-215
legal factors in, 207-208
rules of, 94-95
salaried persons under, 213-214
of salaried positions, 218-223
of salary increases, 216
salary cost, *see* payroll cost
salary curves, 71-74
audit of, 211-213
for company employees, 116-119
comparatio level measure of, 125-137

cost-of-living factor in, 161-162
for high demand occupations, 122
inflationary adjustments in, 101-102, 118-119, 128-129
for salaries surveyed, 114-116
salary formulation on, 71-74
survey data in development of, 102
time synchronization in, 129
salary curve adjustments increase, 161-164
salary decreases, 178-181, 223
salary dispersion, payroll cost vs., 86
salary grades/levels, 67-71
characteristics of, 67-68
in budget planning, 192-195
comparatio ratio for, 126-127, 131
consumer price index vs., 192
differentiation among, 70-71
evaluation among, 68-70
overlapping, 98-99
periodic adjustment of, 68
quotas for, 170
for professional positions, 169-171
salary curves for, 72
salary range vs., 70
in transfers, 26
salary management, 3-7, 94-95
approval system in, 221-223

budgetary, 186–205; *see also*
   budget planning
company size and, 4–7
job evaluation vs., 56–57
salary policy
   budgetary, 187
   comparatio levels and,
      127–128, 131–134,
      138–140
   compensatory adjustments
      as, 120–121
   criteria for, 15–16
   on disclosures, *see* disclo-
      sures
   enforcement of, 22
   formal, 9–11
   in large vs. small company, 9
   model example of, 25–29
   publication of, 15–16
   rigidity in, 22–23
   written or unwritten, 11–15
salary range/spread, 5, 64–67
   actual payments vs., 123,
      124–125
   analysis of, 84–85
   average distribution, 85–86
   compression of, 78, 83
   control of, 94–95
   development of, 160–161
   exceptional cases in, 65–66,
      95–99
   extent of, 59–60, 90–91
   inflationary adjustments in,
      101–102
   merit increases and, 165
   midpoint in, 78–80

older vs. newer employees
   in, 78
overlapping rates in, 74–77,
   98–99
policy on, 10, 21–22, 25–26
promotional increases and,
   171–172, 214–215
salary grades vs., 70
in salary survey reports,
   109–113
single salary vs., 159–160
topheavy, 97–98
salary structure, 64–83
   by grades, 67–71 *see also* sal-
      ary grades/levels
   by ranges, 64–67, *see also*
      salary range/spread
   of small companies, 81–82
salary surveys, 100–114
   area coverage, 102–103, 109
   confidentiality of, 107
   data input into, 105–107
   data resources for, 103–105
   inflationary effects in,
      101–102, 122
   information output of,
      107–114
   job salary coverage in,
      100–101, 109–114
   in salary controls, 211
   sampling problems in,
      121–122
separation, *see* termination
sex discrimination, 97, 212
sick leave pay, 10
small companies
   merit increases in, 149, 151

small companies (*cont.*)
   organizational problems in,
      53
   salary controls in, 6–7, 128
   salary policy in, 9–12, 19
   salary range problems in, 99
   salary structure for, 81–82
   tenure increases in, 169
   updating salaries in, 119–120
standard cost method, 200–203
standard metropolitan statistical area (SMSA), 109
standard salary, 80–81
   actual salary vs., 124–126
   in departmental budgeting,
      201–202
   see also basic salary; mid-
      point salary
starting salaries, 10, 16
   see also minimum salary
supervisors
   in budget planning, 197,
      199, 200–202
   compensable factor rating
      for, 43
   employee performance ap-
      praisal by, 145–149,
      153–154
   job description writing by,
      32
   job evaluation by, 57–58
   pay range of, vs. hourly em-
      ployees, 78, 83
   promotional ranking for,
      36–38
   salary ranges of, 83

temporary assignment pay, 10,
   177–178
temporary promotions, 28
tenure increases, 165, 168–169
termination
   model salary policy for,
      28–29
   recapture of advances at,
      166
   voluntary, 132
time and methods studies,
   190–191
total cash compensation, 106
training salaries, 55, 97
transfers
   downward, 27, 175–176
   geographical, 175–176
   hourly wages to salary, 27,
      174
   lateral, 26–27
   performance appraisals and,
      150–151
   promotions vs., 171, 174–175

unions, 15–16, 61, 163, 226
unit salary method, in budget
   forecasting, 198–199
unwritten salary policy, 11–12

vacation pay, 10
voluntary resignation, pay policy for, 28–29

workforce
   budgetary regulation of,
      190–192

comparatio levels and size of, 132–136

decline in, 132–136, 179

Works of Mencius, The, 37

written salary policy, 12–15, 19–24

written salary records, 223

zero-base budgeting, 191

ALSO OF INTEREST FROM AMACOM

Productivity
A Practical Program for Improving Efficiency
Clair F. Vough with Bernard Asbell

Field-tested system for getting more and better work from employees in a wide range of jobs. Relations between staff and management, technological advances, and the manager's own performance are all given fair, comprehensive consideration.

Compensating Key Executives in the Smaller Company
Theodore Cohn and Roy A. Lindberg
An alternate selection of the Macmillan Executive Program Book Club

Eliminate confusion, counterproductive behavior, and tax problems. Work out the best compensation plans for owners, executives, and employees. Despite guidelines, tax regulations, competition, and inflation, there are plenty of good ways to reward performance.

Financial Management for Small Business
Edward N. Rausch

Managers of small businesses will find this a fact-packed, easy-to-follow "primer" on the basics of financial management from the viewpoint of smaller organizations. Managers can read it from cover to cover or zero in on individual sections that are designed to stand alone as "mini-guides."

Legal Handbook for Small Business
Marc J. Lane
A Main Selection of the McGraw-Hill Book Club

"Extraordinary...an easy-to-read and absolutely essential book for the head of any small business." *Boardroom Reports...* "Recommended" *Library Journal* Written in your kind of language by a practicing attorney.

 A Division of American Management Associations
135 West 50th Street, New York, N.Y. 10020